I0434964

Strategic Studies Institute
and
U.S. Army War College Press

TURKEY-KURDISH REGIONAL
GOVERNMENT RELATIONS
AFTER THE U.S. WITHDRAWAL FROM IRAQ:
PUTTING THE KURDS ON THE MAP?

Bill Park

March 2014

The views expressed in this report are those of the author and do not necessarily reflect the official policy or position of the Department of the Army, the Department of Defense, or the U.S. Government. Authors of Strategic Studies Institute (SSI) and U.S. Army War College (USAWC) Press publications enjoy full academic freedom, provided they do not disclose classified information, jeopardize operations security, or misrepresent official U.S. policy. Such academic freedom empowers them to offer new and sometimes controversial perspectives in the interest of furthering debate on key issues. This report is cleared for public release; distribution is unlimited.

*****

This publication is subject to Title 17, United States Code, Sections 101 and 105. It is in the public domain and may not be copyrighted.

*****

Comments pertaining to this report are invited and should be forwarded to: Director, Strategic Studies Institute and U.S. Army War College Press, U.S. Army War College, 47 Ashburn Drive, Carlisle, PA 17013-5010.

*****

This manuscript was funded by the U.S. Army War College External Research Associates Program. Information on this program is available on our website, *www.StrategicStudies Institute.army.mil*, at the Opportunities tab.

*****

*****

The Strategic Studies Institute and U.S. Army War College Press publishes a monthly email newsletter to update the national security community on the research of our analysts, recent and forthcoming publications, and upcoming conferences sponsored by the Institute. Each newsletter also provides a strategic commentary by one of our research analysts. If you are interested in receiving this newsletter, please subscribe on the SSI website at *www.StrategicStudiesInstitute.army.mil/newsletter*.

FOREWORD

When U.S. forces departed Iraq at the end of 2011, they left behind unresolved problems relating to that country's governance, notably concerning the relationship between the federal authority in Baghdad and the autonomous Kurdistan Regional Government (KRG) in the north. Today, disputes over the territorial delineation of the KRG remain a source of tension, while the discovery of significant reserves of oil and gas within and straddling the borders of the KRG has raised the stakes. Tensions have been heightened still further by the determination of the KRG authorities to pursue an energy policy independent of the central government. This has involved entering into lucrative energy exploration and exploitation agreements with a number of major energy companies, among them the U.S.-based ExxonMobil and Chevron, and moving ahead with an energy partnership with neighboring Turkey involving the construction of direct pipelines across their shared border. Baghdad regards these activities as illegal, and fears that they could be a precursor to Kurdish independence and a break-up of the country. Baghdad also resents Turkey's role in these developments, which has added to the tensions between these two countries that had already emerged as a result of the increasing authoritarianism and Shia sectarianism of the Iraqi government of Prime Minister Nouri al-Maliki.

This monograph, authored by Mr. Bill Park, seeks to explore the ramifications of these developments, both for the region and for U.S. policy and interests. Turkey is a North Atlantic Treaty Organization (NATO) ally, Iraq is a legacy of U.S. policy, and Washington was, in many ways, the midwife for the KRG's initial emergence and subsequent growth. Furthermore, U.S. energy companies are now centrally involved in the evolution of the region and its relationships. Thus, the United States cannot remain indifferent to the march of events in and around Iraq and, whether it likes it or not, will be held at least partly responsible for the outcome. While this monograph makes a contribution to the ongoing debate about the legacy of the past U.S. approach to Iraq, it also performs the valuable service of bringing up to date developments in the region subsequent to the U.S. military withdrawal. To that end, the monograph throws the recent Syrian uprising into the mix. This has intensified sectarian divisions in the Middle East, further pitted Ankara against Baghdad, and additionally raised the specter of the Kurdish question. It has also brought about the deployment of NATO Patriot anti-air batteries into Turkey's southeast, and thrown an additional spotlight on Washington's relationship with its NATO ally, Turkey.

Syria's Kurds are currently seeking to carve an autonomous zone out of that country's chaos, which has aroused the interest of Iraq's Kurds and is profoundly worrying the Turks. Ankara fears that a Syrian Kurdish zone could serve as a refuge and base for the Kurdish Workers Party (PKK), weaken the opposition to Assad, complicate any post-Assad settlement in Syria, and altogether make it harder to keep a lid on its own Kurdish problem. Indeed, Ankara's latest effort to resolve its domestic Kurdish difficulties is surely linked to events in neighboring Syria and Iraq. Thus, Mr. Park's monograph is also a study of the geopolitical ramifications of a Kurdish bid for self-determination, and offers insight into the current struggle in Syria.

Mr. Park's timely monograph addresses a plethora of issues that are vital to a range of U.S. interests, and to the debate over the legacy and purposes of U.S. policy.

DOUGLAS C. LOVELACE, JR.
Director
Strategic Studies Institute and
    U.S. Army War College Press

ABOUT THE AUTHOR

BILL PARK is a Senior Lecturer in the Department of Defence Studies, King's College, London University, and is based at the United Kingdom (UK) Defence Academy, Shrivenham. He is a frequent visitor to Turkey, and has spoken on Turkish affairs at various academic and official workshops and conferences around the world. Mr. Park has appeared as a Turkey expert on British, U.S., Turkish, Russian, French, Iranian and Australian TV and radio, has given written and oral testimony on Turkish issues to both UK Houses of Parliament, and occasionally consults on Turkish issues to various UK government agencies. He serves as a trustee and council member for the British Institute at Ankara, and is an Advisor to the Dialogue Society in London. Mr. Park is the author of journal articles, book chapters, and monographs on a range of Turkish foreign policy issues, including its European Union accession prospects, Turkey and the European Security and Defence Policy (ESDP), the Cyprus problem, Turkey's policies towards Northern Iraq, Turkey-U.S. relations, the Fethullah Gulen movement, and the Ergenekon affair. Among his publications are "Turkey's Policy Towards Northern Iraq: Problems and Prospects," Adelphi Paper No. 374 (International Institute for Strategic Studies, 2005), and *Modern Turkey: People, State and Foreign Policy in a Globalized World* (Routledge, 2011). He is currently conducting a longer-term study of the three-way relationship between Turkey, the United States, and the Kurdish Regional Government in Northern Iraq in the wake of the U.S. troop withdrawal from Iraq.

SUMMARY

The withdrawal of U.S. combat forces from Iraq at the end of 2011 left behind a set of unresolved problems in the relationship between the Kurdistan Regional Government (KRG), and the Federal Government in Baghdad—notably relating to the disputed boundaries of the KRG, and the extent of its autonomy. Tensions have since been compounded by the discovery of significant quantities of oil and gas in the KRG area, and Erbil's pursuit of an energy policy independent of and in opposition to Baghdad. Turkey, uneasy with the increasingly sectarian and authoritarian flavor of the Shia-dominated government in Baghdad, has since moved closer to the KRG, not least with respect to energy issues. This has deepened Turkish-Iraqi tensions still further.

Added to the mix is the increasingly sectarian stand-off in the region as a whole, in large measure as a consequence of Syrian developments, which has further pitted Ankara against Baghdad and its ally, Iran; and the emergence of a bid for autonomy by Syria's Kurds, which has complicated the stance of both Ankara and Erbil towards Syria and towards each other. Washington is in danger of being left behind by the fast-paced events in the region, while the ethnic Kurds of the region may be approaching a decisive moment in their long struggle for self-determination.

TURKEY-KURDISH REGIONAL GOVERNMENT RELATIONS AFTER THE U.S. WITHDRAWAL FROM IRAQ: PUTTING THE KURDS ON THE MAP?

INTRODUCTION

During a question-and-answer session with bureau chiefs in Ankara in early February 2013, the U.S. Ambassador to Turkey Francis J. Riccardione referred to "a lot of divergence" between Washington and Ankara with respect to policy towards Iraq.[1] In this, he was reflecting a growing and increasingly transparent U.S. unease with the close relationship that has evolved between the Turkish government on the one hand and the Kurdistan Regional Government (KRG) of northern Iraq on the other, coupled with and not unrelated to the ever-more fraught relationships that each has with Iraq's central government in Baghdad. Ambassador Riccardione expressed American fears that, "if Turkey and Iraq fail to optimize their economic relations. . . . There could be more violent conflict in Iraq and the forces of disintegration within Iraq could be emboldened." He declared that "a strong Iraqi-Turkish relationship" would be the "optimum outcome" not only for Iraq and Turkey, but for the United States and for the entire region. As a treaty ally of Turkey, friend of the KRG, and as "a partner and non-treaty ally with Iraq," a closer relationship between Turkey and the whole of Iraq is very much an American interest too, and Riccardione made it clear that Washington is endeavoring to persuade Ankara, Baghdad, and the KRG of the mutual benefits of such an outcome. Washington would not interfere or act as an intermediary, but it would "offer confidence and

1

support." The ambassador concluded that, together, Ankara, Baghdad, and Erbil (the KRG's capital) "will profit very greatly. Separately, there are great risks and great dangers."[2]

Energy issues featured strongly in Riccardione's remarks, as they do in the three-way Ankara-Erbil-Baghdad relationship. As a necessary means to achieve what he insisted are the shared interests of all three, he asserted that it is vital that Iraq's feuding political factions agree on a federal hydrocarbons law that would set the terms for the development of Iraq's rich energy resources, and for the distribution of its proceeds. This would give impetus to Iraq's still-shaky economic reconstruction and political stability, and would enable Turkey to have access not just to the estimated 20 percent of Iraq's oil and gas that is located in the Kurdish region, but to the resources of the entire country. It would also enable Turkey to "become a strategic alternative, for all of Iraq, to the straits of Hormuz in getting Iraqi oil and gas out to world markets."[3] This in turn would require the construction of new pipelines that could carry energy from Iraq's fields directly into Turkey, and would reduce vulnerability to any disruption of the "strategic chokepoint" of Hormuz. Turkey and all Iraqis would be the beneficiaries. Indeed, Turkish businesses of all kinds would benefit from greater access to the entire Iraqi economy.

However, the ambassador's comments appear more wishful thinking than realistic analysis. Ankara-Baghdad relations have gone from bad to worse since the end of 2011 with the U.S. military withdrawal from Iraq. Riccardione's comments, which accurately reflect both the perspective and anguish that currently characterizes Washington's view of Iraq, were delivered against the background of yet another ill-tempered exchange of insults between Ankara and

Baghdad, in which Turkish Foreign Minister Ahmet Davutoglu accused Iraqi Prime Minister Nouri al-Maliki of "trying to cover up his failure" by again alleging that Turkey was interfering in Iraq's domestic affairs.[4] Erbil-Baghdad relations have also deteriorated since the end of 2011. Within days of the sensitive Ankara-Baghdad exchange, the Iraqi parliament failed to agree on a national budget as a consequence of differences with Erbil over payments to the KRG for its oil production, a spat rooted in the absence of an agreed national framework for the development of Iraq's hydrocarbons sector.[5] In fact, and notwithstanding Washington's preferences, there is little prospect of a new Iraqi hydrocarbons law appearing over the horizon. Progress on this stalled over 6 years ago, due chiefly to disagreements between Baghdad and Erbil, and in 2007 the KRG pushed ahead with its own hydrocarbons legislation.[6] Within days of Riccardione's warning, Iran delivered a similar message—not to risk the break-up of Iraq by developing too close a relationship with Turkey—to a visiting delegation from the Patriotic Union of Kurdistan (PUK), which is the closest to Iran of the KRG's two ruling parties.[7] There appears to be a surprising degree of alignment between Washington and Tehran with respect to Iraq—a point made by Turkish Ambassador to the U.S. Namik Tan when he noted that "the rhetoric of the U.S. sometimes resembles that of Iran."[8] Washington thus finds itself more in tune with the perspective of an increasingly centralized, authoritarian, sectarian, and Iranian-aligned regime in Baghdad than with those of its North Atlantic Treaty Organization (NATO) ally Turkey or of Erbil.

In fact, alongside or subsequent to the withdrawal of U.S. combat troops from Iraq at the end of 2011, there have been a number of developments which, taken together, are profoundly altering the three-way relationship between Turkey, the KRG, and the federal government in Baghdad. One of these developments is the remarkable transformation of the relationship between Turkey and the KRG. The shift from Ankara's earlier hostile approach to Erbil towards a close economic, political, and even strategic embrace of the KRG began to emerge in 2008-09, before the U.S. troop withdrawal, and has since gathered additional momentum. A second development has been the pronounced cooling of the relationship between Ankara and Baghdad's Shia-dominated government. This is largely a consequence of the increasing centralization of power in Maliki's hands specifically, and Ankara's belief that Maliki's actions are serving only to destabilize and divide Iraq further. Turkey is also uneasy at the extent of Iranian influence in Baghdad.

Perhaps more predictably, the relationship between Erbil and Baghdad has further deteriorated since 2011. Iraq's 2005 constitution, largely drawn up under the supervision of U.S. officials, left numerous loose ends in place. Most notably, both the degree and nature of Erbil's autonomy from Baghdad and the future of the so-called "disputed territories," including the oil-bearing city of Kirkuk but also tracing much of the entire border, or "green line," between Arab Iraq and the KRG, were left decidedly vague. Yet these territories are largely under Kurdish control, in part as an outcome of the relationship between U.S. forces and the Kurds in the immediate aftermath of the 2003 invasion. Iraqis have proven to be incapable of resolving these differences. Indeed, the differences have deepened. The KRG's energetic attempt to develop its energy resources has further inflamed the atmosphere. Erbil has entered exploration agreements with energy majors including U.S. based ExxonMobil and Chevron as well as Anglo-Turkish Genel Energy, French Total, and Russia's Gazprom Neft.[9] Baghdad regards these deals as illegal, as it does Erbil's export of limited amounts of crude oil by truck. Turkey has taken Erbil's side in this dispute. Indeed, Ankara and Erbil are cooperating on the construction of new energy pipelines which will transport the KRG's oil and gas directly to Turkey, potentially bypassing the existing Baghdad-controlled pipeline infrastructure. If implemented, these developments will surely enhance the KRG's scope for de facto economic and indeed political independence from Baghdad. Ankara's readiness to facilitate Erbil's dynamic energy policy has further contributed to the deterioration of its relationship with the federal government in Baghdad. The energy factor has become key to Ankara-Erbil, Erbil-Baghdad, and Ankara-Baghdad relations, and serves to intertwine each of these relationships.

The final key development of note that has occurred since the U.S. military withdrawal from Iraq and that also threatens Ankara-Erbil-Baghdad relationships relates to the so-called Arab Awakening, and particularly its manifestation in Syria. Turkey reacted to the increasingly fierce crackdown against the opposition in Syria by lending its weight to calls for the overthrow of the Damascus, Syria, regime, a move that Damascus; Baghdad; and Tehran, Iran, have been inclined to interpret in sectarian terms. As the Syrian revolt intensified, Turkey's concerns focused increasingly on the Kurds of northern Syria. Largely under the guidance of the Democratic Union Party (*Partiya Yekitiya Demokrat*—PYD), which Turkey believes is aligned with its own separatist Kurdish Workers Party (*Partiya Karkeren Kurdistan*—PKK), Syria's Kurds have established a degree of self-rule in those areas in which they constitute the majority. Ankara fears this could offer an additional springboard for Kurdish terrorist attacks into Turkey, and that it might further complicate its relationship with its own Kurdish population. Furthermore, Syria's Kurds have kept their distance from the main Syrian Arab opposition due to its reluctance to agree to Kurdish autonomy in a post-Assad Syria. The Iraqi Kurdish leadership, at least in the form of its President Massoud Barzani, shares Ankara's mistrust of the PYD, although it favors Syrian Kurdish self-determination. In short, Syrian developments have underscored the sectarian dimension to Ankara-Baghdad relations, and have further highlighted the anomolous position of the region's Kurds.

These still evolving developments, and their interconnectedness, contain potentially serious implications for Washington's regional policies and interests. The United States generally enjoys close relationships with Ankara, Erbil, and Baghdad — the KRG has surely been the most pro-American entity in the region — and will be hard pressed to avoid entanglement in the complexities of their interactions. Some doubt that Baghdad and Erbil can resolve their differences without external mediation, which Washington is best placed to provide. KRG energy minister Ashti Hawrami has called on the United States to mediate the hydrocarbons row between Baghdad and Erbil.[10] Furthermore, considerable political and moral hazard is lurking in Washington's postures towards the two governments. Driven by its fears for Iraq's stability and territorial integrity, the U.S. tilt towards Baghdad is exasperating its Iraqi Kurdish friends and Turkey, and puts it in opposition to the commercial behavior of some of its own energy majors. Nor can Washington expect to evade some political and moral responsibility for the territorial tensions between Erbil and Baghdad. Operations PROVİDE COMFORT and NORTHERN WATCH, the U.S.-led no fly zones over northern Iraq that commenced in 1991, helped create the opportunity for the formation of the KRG, while the U.S.-led overthrow of Saddam Hussein's regime in 2003 was highly instrumental in enabling Erbil to consolidate its autonomy and viability. Washington presided over the drawing up of Iraq's 2005 Constitution, and the subsequent course of the relationship between Iraq's Kurdish and Arab components suggest that it might not be easy for the United States to detach itself from the unresolved territorial and governance issues it left in place.

Furthermore, the legacy of U.S. material and sometimes moral support for Turkey's military campaign against the PKK, and its palpable unease with the possible course of Kurdish self-determination in Iraq, can also appear to pit Washington against minority rights in the region.[11] Any post-Assad Sunni regime that could emerge out of the present chaos in Syria could well turn on its Christian, Druze, and Allawite as well as its Kurdish minorities, adding further scope for acute embarrasment to the mix. It is impossible to hit the right diplomatic note given the region's current turmoil and tensions, but Washington needs to be on guard lest its policies towards — or perhaps its exhaustion with and neglect of — this interlocking set of issues inadvertently strengthen authoritarian and in some instances anti-American regimes in the region, add to sectarian divisions, undermine the development of Iraq's energy industry taken as a whole, upset its best friends in the area, and permit unresolved issues to build up pressures that could explode into violence.

TURKEY AND THE KRG

Massoud Barzani, President of the KRG and leader of the Kurdish Democratic Party (KDP), one of the two leading Iraqi Kurdish parties that have carved up governance of the KRG between them, has over the years repeatedly referred to his aspiration for a fully independent Iraqi Kurdish state.[12] Until relatively recently such comments were greeted with fury in Ankara, where Barzani was famously dismissed as a "tribal chieftain." The deep Turkish unease at the very existence of the KRG, which could be a precursor of a sovereign Kurdish state; the impact this could have on Turkey's own unsettled Kurds; and the belief that the KRG was enabling cross border raids into Turkey by PKK fighters based in the Iraqi Kurdish mountains, have in the past all fed Ankara's hostility. The enlargement of the KRG's territory to incorporate oil-rich Kirkuk was also a Turkish "red line," as it was feared this could vastly improve the viability of an independent Kurdish state. Turkey also championed the Turkmen population of Kirkuk in order to muddy Kurdish claims to the region.[13] Ankara shunned direct contact with the Iraqi Kurdish leadership. Indeed, former (2000-07) Turkish President Ahmet Necdet Sezer even went so far as to refuse to receive his Iraqi counterpart, Jalal Talabani, on the grounds of his concurrent leadership of Iraqi Kurdistan's other major political party, the PUK.[14]

Some leading figures in Turkey's policymaking elite grew increasingly frustrated by this situation. They recognized that the KRG had become a fixture in the region, that it had Washington's blessing, and that its cooperation would be useful in Turkey's struggle with the PKK, given the latter's use of bases located within KRG territory. Furthermore, Turkey's decades-old militarized approach to its domestic Kurdish problem had not succeeded and showed few signs of doing so. They were also frustrated with the slow political progress in Baghdad and, as time passed, its uncertain political sympathies and alignments. Murat Ozcelik, who had served as Ankara's Special Envoy to Iraq until his appointment as Ambassador to Baghdad in 2009, was one such player. There were circles within Turkey's National Intelligence Organization (*Milli Istibahrat Teskilati*, or MIT), such as Emre Taner who became head of the organization in 2005, who similarly sought a change in Ankara's approach. In Erbil, too, some key players were increasingly writing off Baghdad as either an effective or benign political partner, and were on the lookout for alternative sponsors. President Massoud's nephew and now the KRG's prime minister, Nechirvan Barzani, and Barham Salih of the PUK were early proponents of rapprochement with Turkey.[15]

On both sides, such rethinking was given additional impetus as U.S. military withdrawal from Iraq approached. However, nationalist sentiment in Turkey, embraced by many in its ruling Justice and Development Party (JDP) as well as in the bureaucracy and the population at large, made any such policy shift difficult to effect. Chief of the General Staff Yasar Buyukanit (from 2006 until August 2008) was a formidable obstacle to any significant reconsideration of Turkish policy towards the KRG. In contrast, his successor, General Ilker Basbug, shared some of the frustrations of the "forward group" in Ankara and proved far more amenable to a change of tack.[16] More recently, the military's fall from grace as a political player in Ankara, as a consequence of ongoing investigations into its past political activities and of the JDP's unprecedented dominance of the Turkish political scene, have in any case downgraded its capacity to influence Turkish policy.

Yet into 2007 and beyond, the predominant sentiment in Ankara was that the KRG was harboring PKK terrorists and that if neither Erbil or Washington would act against the PKK in their northern Iraqi hideouts, then Turkish forces should be unleashed against them, as they had been throughout the 1990s. Matters came to a head in late-2007 when a PKK attack launched from across the Iraqi border resulted in the deaths of 13 Turkish soldiers. Given the highly charged Turkish atmosphere that ensued, the administration of George W. Bush saw little option but to give the green light to a resumption of cross-border air and ground raids by Turkish security forces, and to facilitate them with the provision of real-time intelligence.[17] Turkey had been denied this option since the 2003 invasion had landed Washington with responsibility for Iraq's security. With the November 2007 understanding, the post-invasion downturn in U.S.-Turkey relations came to an end, and the relationship has been on an upswing almost continuously since. More immediately, however, a substantial Turkish ground incursion in February 2008, named Operation SUN (*Gunes*), produced a confrontation with Iraqi Kurdish forces and American pleas to limit the scale and duration of the operation.[18] Barzani, suspecting the real target was the KRG itself, threatened armed retaliation against Turkish forces.[19] Accompanied by unconvincing denials that it was as a consequence of American pressure, the Turkish force somewhat precipitously withdrew. The PKK remained intact and may even have been emboldened. These events may have further convinced Ankara of the desirability of engaging with Erbil rather than seeking to intimidate it.[20]

Following informal contacts with Barzani in late-2008, the first high level contact he had had with Turkish officials in 4 years, Turkish Foreign Minister Ahmet Davutoglu's October 2009 visit to Erbil paved the way for an intense round of diplomacy and high level visits between Turkey and the Kurdish "quasi-state,"[21] leading to the opening of a Turkish consulate in Erbil in 2010. The relationship has subsequently been fully cemented. As just one indication of how Turkey's recalibration of its approach has gone, in his Kurdish New Year (*Newroz*) address delivered in March 2012, Barzani once again hinted that the time for Iraqi Kurdish self-determination might be drawing closer. He cited the factional infighting in Baghdad and the disregard there of Iraq's constitution, not least with regard to the resolution of the disputed territories.[22] Article 140 of Iraq's 2005 Constitution, which promised the holding of a census and referendum on Kirkuk's future, has not been implemented. The referendum was initially earmarked to take place in 2007, but has been put off indefinitely by Baghdad. Most observers anticipate that a referendum would confirm the desire of a majority of the region's inhabitants to be incorporated into the KRG. For Barzani, Baghdad's obstructiveness on this issue now combined with Maliki's undemocratic, sectarian, centralizing, and unconstitutional behavior, to encourage a reconsideration of the Kurdish commitment to Iraq's territorial integrity and federative structure.[23]

Yet Barzani's comments provoked barely a murmur from Ankara. In fact, in April, just weeks after he made them, he was given the red carpet treatment during a trip to Turkey, where he met with the Republic's president, prime minister, foreign minister and intelligence chief. So far has the relationship now travelled that 2 years later, in the autumn of 2012, President Barzani was an honored guest at Turkey's ruling JDP convention. It is evident that Ankara has come to regard Barzani in particular as a trusted partner and as a leader with political and personal integrity and deep roots in his community.[24] Enthusiasts for the relationship on the Kurdish side, such as KRG Prime Minister Nechirvan Barzani, now use the term "strategic" to describe their relationship.[25] Turkey's once menacing policy of keeping the KRG at arms lengths has melted away. Ankara seems to have dissolved some of its own "red lines."

There are additional factors behind this paradigm shift in Ankara's relationship with the KRG. The growth of cross-border trade predated the improvement in the political atmosphere, and dates back at least to the lifting of sanction on Iraq following the overthrow of the Ba'athist regime. Although available figures vary slightly, trade with the KRG now accounts for well over half of Turkey's trade with Iraq as a whole, which is Turkey's second or third largest trading partner. Up to 80 percent of Turkish exports to Iraq are to the KRG, and around 80 percent of consumer goods available in the KRG are of Turkish origin. Tens of thousands of Turkish citizens work or have established businesses in Kurdish Iraq, many of them Turkish Kurds. Indeed, the potential economic benefits of the KRG's booming economy to Turkey's impoverished and predominantly Kurdish-inhabited southeast is not lost on Turkey's ruling JDP, which is engaged in a competition for votes in the region with the pro-Kurdish Peace and Democracy Party (*Baris ve*

Demokrasi Partisi — BDP). Almost half of all businesses established in the KRG originate in Turkey. Turkish companies are heavily engaged in construction, engineering, transportation, retail, banking, other areas of the service sector, and, of course, energy. Turkish religious groups have established schools and a university in the region.

Turkish foreign policy has followed its trade patterns and reflects the importance Turkey's current government attaches to "soft power" as an instrument or precursor to its influence. It also constitutes an expression of Foreign Minister Ahmet Davutoglu's "zero problems" and dialogue-based approach to neighborhood diplomacy. Indeed, his May 2009 elevation to that post was itself a factor in Turkey's apparent paradigm shift in its approach to the KRG, although he was already a prime foreign policy mover in his former position as Prime Minister Erdogan's foreign policy advisor. All in all, the KRG is on the way to becoming part of a Turkish "near abroad," politically and economically. Some might regard this as a manifestation of Turkey's "neo-Ottoman" bid to establish itself as a key regional player.

Ankara has also come to appreciate that prospects for its struggle with the PKK and for its bid to win the hearts and minds of Turkey's Kurdish voters might be enhanced by Erbil's cooperation. In his April 2012 trip to Turkey, Barzani reiterated his frequently-voiced call for the PKK to end its armed campaign, promised to pressure the PKK to end its cross-border raids into Turkey, and declared that he "will not allow the PKK to prevail in the [KRG] region"[26] — all music to Ankara's ears, although it was hardly the first time Turks have heard such utterances from Iraq's Kurdish leaders. Both the PKK and the BDP immediately warned Barzani against involving himself in Turkey's Kurdish problem on behalf of Ankara, seeking to downplay the impact his intervention might have.[27] Barzani and other Iraqi Kurdish leaders have also declared their support for the dialogue between Ankara and Turkey's Kurds that has emerged in recent months. This follows the failure of the 2009 initiative to address politically Turkey's Kurdish problem that, by 2011, had run into the ground.[28] The more recent effort has involved engaging with the jailed PKK leader Abdullah Ocalan, but Turkey presumably hopes that the soothing words of Iraq's Kurdish leaders will also hold some sway.

For its part, the KRG leadership certainly wishes to minimize the PKK's provocations against Ankara (and Tehran) launched from KRG territory, and to see an end to Turkey's raids into KRG territory in pursuit of PKK targets. It has long been a Turkish demand that the KRG authorities take military steps to expel or weaken the PKK fighters based in northern Iraq, and the Iraqi Kurdish failure to comply has for just as long been a source of frustration to Turkey. However, Ankara now appears to have concluded that it is unreasonable to expect the KRG to be willing or even able to physically confront PKK forces in their remote hideouts in the Kandil Mountains of northern Iraq. Iraqi Kurdish appeals to the PKK to end violence, their silence in the face of Turkey's cross border raids, and any intelligence and other assistance made available to Turkey's security forces, now seem to be sufficient if not entirely satisfactory to Ankara.[29]

TURKEY AND BAGHDAD

Along with Barzani, Iraqi Prime Minister Nouri al-Maliki was also invited to the JDP's autumn 2012 convention. Unlike Barzani, Maliki chose not to attend, which symbolized the cooling of the Ankara-Baghdad relationship. This is not a development Ankara had intended. Even as it moved closer to Erbil, Ankara's overall stance towards Iraq remained what it had been since 2003 — to shore up Baghdad, partly in order to minimize the scope for Iraqi Kurdish independence, but also in the hope of stabilizing Iraq and countering Iranian influence there. From the very beginning, Ankara regarded full Sunni Arab engagement with Iraq's political reconstruction as a vital means to these ends. Thus, it was instrumental in limiting the Sunni boycott of the 2005 elections, and in coaxing Sunni participation in the 2009 provincial and 2010 parliamentary elections in Iraq. Ankara had since 2003 sought to cultivate relationships with all the country's factions, including the Sadr Movement, which although Shia and close to Iran is also lukewarm towards Maliki and in favor of greater Shia-Sunni unity in Iraq. In 2008, Ankara and Maliki's first government agreed to establish a High Level Strategic Cooperation Council, and bilateral trade and political dialogue between the two capitals grew apace. In the 2010 elections, Ankara's preference for the Ayad Allawi's al-Iraqiya non-sectarian bloc was clear, perhaps inadvisably so, given the eventual outcome. Although Allawi's bloc gained the (marginally) largest share of the popular vote and of parliamentary seats and did indeed attract large Sunni but also Shia and even Turkmen support, it was Maliki who eventually emerged at the head of a coalition government in December 2010. Turkey's aim was to encourage power-sharing, good governance, economic reconstruction, and stability in Iraq, not to favor one faction over another. Furthermore, its Iraq policy fitted with its wider endeavor to forge a more active and cooperative role in the region.[30]

Yet, despite these efforts, by January 2012 Maliki was condemning Turkey's "interference" in Iraq's affairs after Prime Minister Erdogan had warned him against stoking sectarian divisions in the country. Erdogan's intervention had been prompted by the attempted arrest of Iraqi's Sunni Vice-President Tariq al-Hashemi on the very day that U.S. Defense Secretary Leon Panetta was overseeing the formal end of the American military presence in Iraq. The war of words between Baghdad and Ankara continued to deteriorate, particularly once Hashemi was granted protection by Turkey, after first receiving sanctuary in Iraqi Kurdistan.[31] Maliki described Turkey as "hostile" towards Iraq and accused Ankara of pursuing a sectarian agenda.[32] For his part, Hashemi declared that "hopes for early political solutions no longer exist" in Iraq,[33] for which he laid the blame at Maliki's door. Turkey's perspective accords with Hashemi's. Hashemi has also insisted that the refuge Ankara had offered him was based not on sectarian considerations but as a result of Turkey's commitment to Iraqi democratization.[34] He subsequently has been given five death sentences in absentia by Iraqi courts on terrorism charges.

Relations between Ankara and Baghdad have since progressively deteriorated. In January 2012, the Turkish Embassy in Baghdad was subjected to a rocket attack. In May 2012, Baghdad called in Turkey's ambassador to protest that Turkey's Basra and Mosul consuls were meddling in Iraq's domestic politics.[35] In

July 2012, Baghdad even threatened to report Turkey to the United Nations (UN) Security Council for violations of Iraqi airspace as a consequence of Turkish air strikes against PKK targets within the KRG area, an activity which Iraq had hitherto generally tolerated.[36] Similarly, in October 2012, Baghdad raised the issue of the presence of Turkish military bases on Iraqi soil, albeit within the KRG zone, an arrangement which had long been tolerated by successive Iraqi governments.[37] Baghdad even considered deploying non-Kurdish Iraqi troops on the border with Turkey in order to obstruct Turkish ground incursions.[38] There have also been persistent rumors that Erdogan promised Barzani that Turkey would offer protection to the KRG in the event of an attack by Baghdad's forces.[39] The war of words between Ankara and Baghdad has been given additional impetus by other developments in the region, notably Turkey's burgeoning energy relationship with the KRG and events in Syria.

Maliki's move against Hashemi, which included the arrest or marginalization of other leading Sunni politicians, appeared in Ankara as a challenge to power-er sharing and pluralism in Iraq, which Ankara sees as offering the best hope for political stability in the country; and as a Shia—and perhaps indirectly Iranian—bid for power and predominance in Iraq. Ankara had long been anxious about Maliki's centralizing, authoritarian, and seemingly sectarian inclinations. Maliki has progressively subverted or bypassed the governing institutions put in place since 2003, and has concentrated power in his own hands by, for example, placing the military, the paramilitary special forces, and Iraq's national intelligence forces under his direct control.[40] Ankara has also remained close to some of Iraq's Sunni elements, including those like Hashemi who had come to favor greater regional autonomy in Iraq as a counterweight to Maliki's increasing autocracy.[41] Nor is Turkey happy about the degree of influence it believes Iran wields in Maliki's Iraq. In this context, the arrest warrant for Hashemi represented something of a last straw for Turkey. Turkish "zero problem" diplomacy had collided with Iraq's fractious, fragile, and sectarian politics, although trade relations between the two neighbors have continued to prosper.

ERBIL-BAGHDAD RELATIONS

More predictable has been the continuing tension between Erbil and Baghdad. Although the Kurdish bloc had supported Maliki in preference to Ayad Allawi's bid to head the government and has held on to key, if increasingly notional, federal government posts (most notably Jalal Talabani's incumbency as president and Hoshyar Zebari's as foreign minister) before long there was mounting Kurdish frustration with the Maliki government's disregard for the power-sharing foundation stone of the coalition and for the provisions of the constitution. In fact, Barzani had played a key role in brokering the November 2010 deal, known as the "Erbil Agreement" that led to Maliki's second spell as prime minister. This obliged Maliki to sign up to a 15-point list specifically designed to limit his accretion of power, a trend that had already been amply demonstrated during his spell as prime minister before the March 2010 elections. Maliki has subsequently almost entirely ignored the terms of this agreement, although at the time of this writing, it has as yet proved impossible to put together enough support for a no-confidence vote in Iraq's Council of

Representatives. Barzani has repeatedly condemned Maliki's centralization of power and has especially singled out his increasing domination of federal Iraq's security apparatus. He has criticized Washington's readiness to supply arms to Iraq's military, especially F-16s, which Barzani fears could be used against the Kurds, and has explicitly supported autonomous arrangements for Iraq's Sunni provinces.[42] Barzani's April 2012 and subsequent threats to hold a referendum on Kurdish independence are a response to Maliki's autocratic tendencies as much as or more than they are a reflection of ultimate Kurdish aspirations.

Since the KRG came into being, a major source of difference with Baghdad has been the KRG's claim that the governorate of Kirkuk and other heavily Kurdish populated areas along the "Green Line" border with the remainder of Iraq should be attached to the KRG. The entry of the Kurdish *peshmerga* into many of these areas ahead of or alongside U.S. troops in 2003, where for the most part they remain, appeared to enhance Kurdish prospects of success, as did the strong Kurdish political, administrative, economic, and security presence that was soon established in these "disputed" territories. Article 140 of the 2005 Constitution, which the Kurds played a major role in devising and Sunni Arabs almost none, undertook to "normalize" the disputed areas by reversing earlier "Arabization" programs. Recently settled Arabs would be encouraged to return to their places of origin and displaced Kurds and other minorities would be allowed to return. This was to be followed by a census, which would pave the way for a referendum to be held by December 2007. Exactly which territories were disputed and who had the right of return was left vague. In any case, the federal government holds the responsibility for implementing these measures, and it has shown itself unwilling to do so. Neither Erbil nor Baghdad appears likely to back down on its claim to these mixed population areas.

Tensions between Kurds and local Arab, Turkmen, and other ethnic groups in Kirkuk, the surrounding countryside, and other disputed territories of mixed demographic makeup remain high. Peace was initially maintained by joint U.S. Army, Iraqi Army, and Kurdish *peshmerga* patrols, but cooperation broke down in the wake of the American withdrawal. In the absence of U.S. forces, the risk of direct confrontation between the Kurdish security forces and those of other ethnic groups or the federal government has become serious.[43] The disputed areas remain a flashpoint, as most recently evidenced by the violent clash between the Kurdish *peshmerga* and Baghdad's Djila, or Tigris, Operational Command. This unit was formed by Maliki in mid-2012 in his capacity as Iraq's Commander-in-Chief and justified on the basis of the requirement to provide security in and around Kirkuk—or to provide protection to Arab and other non-Kurdish communities from Kurdish forces in the area. This move was interpreted by the Kurds as a challenge to their position, and they demanded the force to be removed and disbanded. The *pershmerga* presence in the region was augmented. A three-star U.S. General was highly instrumental in defusing the tension, but Kurdish and Iraqi federal forces remain in place and confronting each other,[44] as they do on the Syrian border following a confrontation there in July 2012.[45]

Maliki argues that federal Iraqi forces have the right and responsibility to ensure security for all Iraqis throughout the country, including in the disputed territories and along Iraq's international borders.

This stance helps swing Arab nationalist opinion, Sunni as well as Shia, to his side. Furthermore, Kurdish uncertainties about the outcome of a referendum, and differences between the KDP and the PUK as to which of them might take the lead role in various of the claimed areas, has in practice dampened Kurdish urgency. Furthermore, studies conducted by the UN Assistance Mission for Iraq (UNAMI), which commenced in December 2007 but whose findings were never made public, largely served to muddy the more maximalist Kurdish demands.[46] As a consequence of these factors, no referendum has been held, and the territories remain "disputed' — or, as Barzani and other Kurds prefer to call them, "detached." Yet there has been little tempering of Kurdish rhetoric in support of their territorial claims, and Maliki's unwillingness to deliver the constitutional promises has been a major factor in Barzani's increasing frustration with Baghdad. The Kurds' best opportunity to seize Kirkuk and other disputed territories for themselves was in 2003 in the immediate aftermath of the U.S.-led invasion. Now, in the absence of a referendum, the KRG cannot acquire them by peaceful means and, with the passage of time, the capacity of Baghdad's security forces to deny any forceful Kurdish acquisition of the territories may grow. Mooted U.S. arms sales will further enhance Baghdad's relative and absolute military capacity vis-á-vis Erbil. The territorial issue remains a potential flashpoint.

In June 2013, Maliki paid a visit to Erbil in the latest attempt to patch up the government's multifaceted quarrel with the Kurds in the north. Barzani described these talks as the "last chance" to resolve the differences between Erbil and Baghdad, and once again appeared to threaten Kurdish secession should they fail.[47] The visit resulted in the establishment of seven joint committees to address the energy, budgetary, territorial, border crossing responsibilities, and other differences that have brought Baghdad and Erbil to the brink of armed conflict.[48] The issues look intractable, and there seems to be little likelihood of an early agreement, if any agreement at all.

THE ENERGY NEXUS: A GAME CHANGER?[49]

Kirkuk lies at the center of what was once Iraq's biggest oil and gas field and has been heavily exploited since its discovery in the 1920s and neglected as a consequence of the more recent conflicts and sanctions. It nevertheless continues to hold considerable reserves. The twin pipelines that transport oil from Kirkuk to the Turkish Mediterranean port at Ceyhan are controlled by the federal Iraqi government. Repeatedly sabotaged, they are currently operating far below capacity and are in dire need of refurbishment. Although the Kurds have insisted that their claim to Kirkuk and the surrounding countryside derives from its historical association with ethnic Kurds and the current demographic balance, Iraq's Arabs and—in the past—Turkey have been inclined to interpret the Kurdish claim to the region as a bid to ensure the economic wherewithal for greater independence.

The current constitutionally-sanctioned arrangement is that the KRG receives 17 percent of Iraq's national budget, which is roughly in line with the KRG's percentage share of Iraq's population. As part of this arrangement, any earnings from oil and gas fields within the KRG's territory should be transferred to Iraq's national budget. In practice, the arrangement has been fraught with difficulty. In continuing disputes over both the KRG's deliveries of energy and over Baghdad's liability to pay, Baghdad has repeatedly suspended payment, and Erbil has just as repeatedly suspended deliveries. Erbil's resort to trucking oil, at below market prices, across its borders into Turkey and Iran as a consequence of the payments dispute cannot serve as a long-term export solution for the KRG, and even less so for those companies that are or soon will be in a position to bring oil to the surface from the substantial fields that have been newly discovered within the KRG's borders. In any case, Baghdad regards these exports as illegal. Any payments that Baghdad does make to Erbil—as a result of an agreement made in September 2012, for example, but one that soon collapsed—are intended to cover the costs of exploration and production in the KRG's new fields, but not the profits of the oil companies there.

It is believed by the KRG that Baghdad should be content with the dynamic approach adopted by Erbil to the exploration and exploitation of new oil and gas fields in territory under Kurdish control. Iraq's total national revenue would increase as the north's energy resources are exploited and exported. However, Erbil insists that it has the legal right to initiate the development of new fields within the areas it controls, and has signed around 50 so-called Production Sharing Contracts (PSCs) with energy companies, most of them small. The terms on offer theoretically permit the international energy companies operating in the KRG to retain around 20 percent of the profits, as opposed to the 1 or 2 percent that Iraq's fee-per-barrel-of-oil-produced service contracts might typically yield. The estimates of energy reserves in the KRG area has substantially increased since Erbil decided to enter into its own exploration agreements, and, when combined with the investment-friendly KRG operating environment, there has been no shortage of international energy companies prepared to take a risk against the uncertain political environment. Indeed, although such estimates are notoriously varying and contingent, it is possible and even likely that around 30 percent of Iraq's oil reserves lie in the Kurdish north of the country. If correct, the KRG alone would be the world's 10th most oil-rich country (Iraq as a whole ranks second), roughly on a par with Nigeria or Libya. Its actual production could very soon match that of Azerbaijan.

However, Baghdad's interpretation of Iraq's ambiguous and vague Constitution is that, as the federal government, it alone has the right to enter into negotiations with international energy companies concerning the exploitation of Iraqi national resources. In part, then, Iraq's energy disputes can essentially be seen as disputes about the nature of the country's federal arrangements and the degree of its decentralization — or even about Kurdish secession altogether. Baghdad's suspicions are strengthened by the fact that some of the PSCs Erbil has negotiated cover territory that it controls but that lie within the disputed territories rather than within the KRG's recognized boundaries. It is also concerned that the terms of agreements entered into by Erbil are not aligned with those that Baghdad negotiates. Baghdad's response to what it regards as the KRG's illegal activities has been to threaten to blacklist any energy company that does business with the KRG from bidding for contracts in Iraq's larger southern fields.

This approach was fine when the companies doing business in northern Iraq were small and unlikely to obtain much of a stake in Iraq's southern fields. However, the stakes were considerably raised as a consequence of the U.S. oil major company ExxonMobil's surprising decision in November 2011 to sign an oil and gas exploration agreement with Erbil. Baghdad was obliged to implement its threat by excluding Exxon from a bidding contest in Iraq's southern oil fields in retaliation, but for contractual reasons it could do nothing about Exxon's existing stake in southern Iraq's West Qurna 1 field. In a further blow to Baghdad, the exploration blocs that Exxon had acquired in its 20-year deal with Erbil include fields located in the disputed areas. Exxon is expected to start drilling in mid-2013. Although in early-2013 it appeared that Exxon might be prepared to sacrifice its agreement with the KRG to exact a better offer from Baghdad for its southern operations,[50] the company has subsequently been reported as having entered into a KRG exploration agreement with a Turkish partner.[51] In July 2012 ExxonMobil was followed by another U.S. oil giant, Chevron, when it acquired an interest in two exploration blocks in KRG territory; this was, in turn, followed within weeks by the French oil major company Total and by the Russian company, Gazprom. Like ExxonMobil these companies too seemed undeterred by Baghdad's threats to exclude them from contracts in southern Iraq—in fact, Chevron has no stake in Iraq's south[52] and has since acquired a third exploration block in the north.[53] Doing business with the KRG is far more lucrative and less frustrating than dealing with Iraq's federal government. It is also possible that the oil majors have calculated that, in the longer term, a deal between Erbil and Baghdad will be struck because the riches at stake are too high—this is certainly the view of Tony Haywood, former British Petroleum (BP) Chief Executive and now Chief Executive of Genel Energy, which is a major energy investor in Iraqi

Kurdistan.[54] They may also calculate that Iraq will find itself unable to operate effectively without access to the capital and know-how of the oil majors.

Turkey Eyes the KRG's Energy Resources.

BP's recent expression of interest in reviving the Kirkuk oilfield infrastructure is very much at the mercy of the Kurds who, given the physical presence of Kurdish forces and their substantial administrative control over the region, are well-placed to sabotage any initiatives from which they are excluded.[55] Unsurprisingly, the KRG reacted negatively when in January 2013, BP announced it would make an initial short-term investment in the parts of the Kirkuk field that lie within the formally Baghdad-administered area, and that negotiations with Baghdad were still ongoing.[56] Erbil declared this step as "illegal and unconstitutional." The KRG simultaneously defended as legal and constitutional its decision a few days earlier to permit Genel Energy to export oil to world markets directly via Mersin in Turkey, bypassing Baghdad.[57] Hitherto, trucked exports of crude to Turkey had been in return for refined products, given the KRG's lack of refinery capacity. Baghdad's reaction to Genel's export venture was to threaten to sue the company and to cut the KRG's 17 percent share of Iraq's national budget,[58] a move that the February 2013 debates surrounding the Iraqi national budget suggests would be popular with Iraq's Arab political leaders.

The KRG's problem—and that of the companies involved there—is how to export the oil and gas which is now being extracted in limited quantities, but production of which is scheduled to soar. In the absence of a solution to this problem, the investments made by the energy companies will have been in vain, and the energy reserves that have been discovered there will remain unavailable to the world market. It would be helpful if Erbil's continuing legal and political differences with Baghdad over production, export, and payment could be resolved by the time production begins apace in 2014. If these difficulties, and the clashing territorial claims around Kirkuk, could be settled, then a restoration of the Kirkuk infrastructure and the Kirkuk-Ceyhan pipelines — presumably with BP as the most likely contractor — would be in Erbil's interest too. However, any such resolution appears to be a very long way off. The KRG's limited storage, pipeline, and refining infrastructure compounds Erbil's problem.

Given the fractious relationship with Baghdad, access to Turkey's market and its energy infrastructure presents itself as the more desirable option for the KRG. Turkey is the most obvious export route for Iraqi Kurdish energy, and its hunger for energy makes it the KRG's most obvious market. Kurdish oil and gas would also feed into Ankara's aspiration to develop as an energy hub. Genel Energy is the largest of a number of Turkey-based companies engaged in the KRG's energy sector. More significant is the growing involvement of the Turkish state. The direct exportation via Turkey of Genel's crude oil could only have taken place with Ankara's approval. More dramatic was the announcement in May 2012 of an agreement between Ankara and Erbil, following a visit to Ankara by KRG Prime Minister Nechirvan Barzani[59] and made without Baghdad's involvement, that two new pipelines could be constructed to carry gas and oil directly across the border into Turkey.[60] Although Turkey has yet to formally commit to plans to run the pipelines directly across the border, they were first publicly announced by the KRG's Natural Resources Minister Ashti Hawrami at an energy conference in Erbil in the presence of a large Turkish delegation headed by Ankara's Energy Minister Taner Yildiz. Baghdad was not represented. In June 2013, Hawrami announced that an oil pipeline from the KRG to Turkey would be completed by September 2013, that the Anglo-Turkish company Genel Energy would begin exporting oil via the pipeline in 2014, and that gas exports to Turkey would begin in 2016.[61] The oil pipeline is planned to reach the border alongside the Baghdad-controlled Kirkuk-Ceyhan pipeline at Fish Khabur, into which it could in principle feed in order that its throughput could be monitored by Baghdad. However, there would also be the option of constructing an entirely new stretch of line into Turkey, or joining it to the existing pipeline at a new monitoring station closer to the Turkish border — which could be controlled by Erbil rather than Baghdad — or even across the border inside Turkish territory.[62] Although the KRG section of the pipeline is expected to be operated by Erbil, it is also assumed that the Kurds will take only their 17 percent of the proceeds, and transfer the remainder to Baghdad's coffers. A feasibility study for the gas pipeline has already been commissioned.[63] There is also the option of a reversible-flow pipeline that could pump Kirkuk oil southwards to Basra, or southern oil northwards to Kirkuk and on to Turkey, and some limited pumping is apparently now viable again after the damage caused by U.S. bombing and sabotage.[64] In spite of this, Baghdad has invested little in developing this element of its infrastructure, notwithstanding Turkish expressions of interest in helping develop Iraq's north-south pipeline infrastructure.[65]

It is possible that the new pipeline plans represent an attempt by Turkey to put pressure on Baghdad. However, there can be little doubt that Ankara is frustrated with the slow pace of Iraq's energy policy and the absence of a federal energy law, and that it is impatient to exploit the opportunities offered by the KRG. As former U.S. Ambassador to Turkey James Jeffrey put it:

> Sooner or later, hydrocarbons will be exported out of northern Iraq. The question is whether that would be done in cooperation with Baghdad, and thus reinforcing the unity and federal system in Iraq, or whether that would be done in another, maybe less helpful, way.[66]

He went on to say, "A major reason behind the failure has been Baghdad's lack of cooperation, including not paying the second [installment] of payments to the companies in the north."[67] National elections are due in 2014 and could be held earlier still. Barzani has reportedly asserted that the Kurds of Iraq will go their own way should Maliki remain in power after 2014.[68] There is little reason to assume that the task of assembling coalitions in Baghdad that are inclusive of its sectarian and ethnic groups is likely to become easier in the future. Iraq's Sunni provinces might also edge towards greater autonomy from a Shia dominated and centralizing Baghdad. When added to the persisting sectarian violence in Arab Iraq, the omens for the consolidation of Iraqi democracy and the establishment of stable governance are not good. Furthermore, Shia dominated Iraq's increasing ties to Iran are unmistakeable and possibly irreversible. In short, reasons for optimism regarding Iraq's future desirability as a regional partner, for Turkey or for Erbil, seem somewhat thin.

The year 2014 coincides with the likelihood that the oil majors operating within the KRG area will be ready to export energy commercially. Only time will tell how far Turkey is prepared to go in the pursuit of an energy relationship with Erbil which would both enhance the KRG's financial independence from Baghdad and symbolize its political estrangement, but the clock is clearly ticking.[69] If, within a very few years from now, Maliki or some other equally awkward political leader is in power in Iraq, a federal hydrocarbons agreement remains in abeyance, and Ankara (and Erbil) are confronted with the choice of enabling the export of commercial quantities of energy or of seeing the energy majors such as Exxon and Chevron wind down their activities in the KRG, Turkey might take the risk. Indeed, the exigencies of pipeline construction might push them towards a still earlier decision.[70] Energy is now widely regarded as a truly transformative factor in this three-way set of relationships between Ankara, Erbil, and Baghdad. In essence, it has brought Ankara closer still to Erbil, and distanced both from Baghdad. There is an increasing sense that the KRG's energy resources could propel profound geopolitical changes in the region.

The Iraqi government clearly believes Turkey has already gone too far in its relationship with Erbil. Unsurprisingly, Baghdad reacted angrily to an unannounced visit to Kirkuk by Turkish Foreign Minister Ahmet Davutoglu in August 2012. Davutoglu travelled to Kirkuk directly from Erbil without first informing the Iraqi government, according to Baghdad. Although the primary purpose of Davutoglu's trip was to meet with and reassure the city's Turkmen population and thus could not be construed as a show of support for Kurdish claims to the city,

Maliki nevertheless accused Turkey of treating the KRG as an independent state, and threatened a review of Baghdad's relationship with Ankara.[71] In November 2012, Baghdad offered no explanation for its expulsion of the Turkish Petroleum Corporation (*Turkiye Petrolleri A.O.* – TPAO) from an oil exploration deal in Iraq's south.[72] In the following month, Baghdad even refused permission for the private jet carrying Turkish Energy Minister Taner Yildiz to land at Erbil airport. Although it claimed the reason was technical, the incident came amidst reports that Yildiz was about to finalize the pipeline deal with Erbil.[73] The indications are that Erbil is already within Ankara's, far more than Baghdad's, orbit, and that the likely future direction of travel will cement this. What might be the implications of this development?

WASHINGTON'S APPROACH

As already noted, the November 2007 agreement between the Bush administration and Prime Minister Erdogan whereby Washington undertook to provide "real time actionable intelligence" in support of Turkey's attacks against PKK bases in northern Iraq, heralded the warming of a relationship that had entered a deep chill since the 2003 U.S.-led invasion of Iraq. The agreement served as a reminder to the KRG that Washington's relationship with Turkey enjoyed high priority, and encouraged Erbil's opening to Ankara. The December 2008 Status of Forces agreement between the Bush administration and Baghdad led inexorably to the end of 2011 withdrawal of U.S. military forces from Iraq, after it had proved impossible to agree on terms with Baghdad that would enable some U.S. forces to remain. This intensified Erbil's anxiety, especially given the unresolved differences between Erbil and Baghdad over the disputed territories and the nature of the Iraqi federation.[74] Iraqi Kurdish unease had already been sparked by President Obama's November 2010 request that Iraqi President Talabani, a Kurd, give up his post for Ayad Allawi to take over.[75] Iraq's Kurds detect the possibility that Washington might sacrifice them, which would not be a new experience for them. Simultaneously, the likelihood that a Shia dominated Iraq would move closer to Iran made Ankara uneasy. These anxieties gave additional impetus to the relaxation of Turkish-KRG relations, as both parties sought to better position themselves in what was seen as the void left behind by the American departure.

Had Turkey and Iraq been able to maintain a functioning relationship, the situation might have been more manageable. Turkey could have offered Iraq an alternative to political and diplomatic over-dependency on Iran and a shared desire to limit the KRG's autonomy, while the KRG would have been left in little doubt regarding its limited scope to pursue more expansive objectives. However, the political and diplomatic fallout between Ankara and Baghdad, the increasing energy significance of the KRG area, and the sectarian rifts that have become ever more evident in the region, have undermined the prospects of such a benign outcome. These developments have also demonstrated that Washington's commitment to Baghdad, notwithstanding Maliki's increasing authoritarianism and sectarianism, and to combating any apparent threats to Iraq's territorial integrity, are no less a determinant of the U.S. stance than its alliance with Turkey and its residual and moral responsibility to Iraqi Kurdistan. This has produced a somewhat unanticipated situation in which Washington, which, in general, is pleased with the Turkey-KRG rapprochement, is nevertheless uncomfortable with some of its details and nervous about its possible implications for Iraq's territorial integrity and for the stability of the region.[76]

This is most evident with respect to the KRG's energy deals. Washington has advised U.S. energy companies that they should first clear with Baghdad any agreements they might be contemplating with the KRG, citing the legal uncertainty surrounding such agreements, although Washington also insists that it cannot directly interfere with commercial decisions.[77] Furthermore, although Washington has been coy about admitting it, the United States has been putting pressure on Turkey to temper its energy relationship with Erbil, reminding Ankara that its approach threatens to contradict Turkey's own opposition to an independent Iraqi Kurdistan.[78] The Turkish response is that it cannot be expected to ignore the existence of such considerable energy resources on its doorstep, particularly in light of the fact that almost 50 energy companies, including a number from the United States, are actively engaged there.[79] Ankara also sides with Erbil in rejecting Baghdad's view that the KRG's energy deals with third parties, including Turkey and the oil majors, are illegal.[80] In effect, Washington is now more concerned than is Ankara with the implications for Iraq's territorial integrity of the KRG's drive to develop its energy sector.[81]

It is similarly noteworthy that the Obama administration appears determined to proceed with a major package of arms sales and training programs with Maliki's government, even though Sunni politicians and even the then U.S. Ambassador to Iraq James

Jeffrey have expressed their disquiet.[82] The deal includes the purchase of main battle tanks and 36 F16 fighter jets due for delivery between 2014 and 2018.[83] President Barzani has expressed his fears that the F16s in particular could be used against Iraqi Kurdistan, and believes Washington to be mistaken in its continued support of the Maliki government.[84] Although some have detected an element of hyperbole in Barzani's comments, there is some risk in Washington's stance and some substance to Barzani's concerns given the current military standoff between Kurdish and government forces around Kirkuk and elsewhere, the unresolved political differences between Baghdad and Erbil, and the long history of Arab-Kurdish conflict and violence in Iraq. Furthermore, Barzani's comments were made in the context of a reported failure to obtain the security guarantees he sought during his April 2012 Washington visit.[85]

To some extent, Washington's position might be explained by a degree of inertia in the American approach to Iraq. Although Iraq has not been a priority for the Obama administration, Washington has embraced the legacy of the extraordinary U.S. commitment to Iraq of the recent past and has sustained the direct personal relationship with Maliki.[86] It has seemed content to allow the inherited political commitment to the Maliki government to dictate its approach. In any case, there is a widespread view in the United States that the KRG has achieved as much as it can reasonably expect, and that independence was not, and should not be, an option. Washington under Obama also appears aware of U.S. limitations in Iraq, and indeed in the wider region and beyond, is less intent on taking initiatives, and is particularly inclined to take account of Ankara's perspectives.[87] Its behavior suggests a belief that there is little it can or should do beyond encouraging dialogue and consensus, although it is highly likely that Washington is applying pressure behind the scenes.

MOVING PARTS, UNKNOWN UNKNOWNS, AND PARADIGM SHIFTS: TIME FOR A STATE OF KURDISTAN?

However, the risks and opportunities in the region are now looking profoundly different from what they were at end of 2011. The Arab Spring, particularly its manifestation in Syria, has introduced new and unanticipated elements into the already complicated Ankara-Erbil-Baghdad triangular relationship. First, the sectarian dimension of the Syrian turmoil, and the manner in which this has both reflected and stoked sectarian schisms in the wider region, have served to deepen the rift between Turkey on the one hand and Baghdad and Tehran on the other. Second, the position of Syria's Kurdish minority, which amounts to around 10 percent of its population, has added further complexity to Turkey's relationships with the KRG and with its own Kurds, and has brought into greater focus the predicament of the region's Kurds. Iraq's Kurds are at the center of this monograph, but their fate is very much entangled with the fates of their Kurdish cousins in Turkey, Syria, and, indeed, Iran. In being denied a state of their own, the Kurds can be said to have been losers in history's evolution thus far. Could this be about to change? Might the map of the region be redrawn to accommodate a Kurdish state? A number of seasoned commentators have ventured the argument that the prospect of eventual Kurdish independence has been strengthened immeasurably

35

as a consequence of regional developments such as those in Iraq and Syria.[88] Even an Iraqi newspaper editor said to be very close to Maliki has speculated whether the time has come for a negotiated separation of Arabs and Kurds in Iraq,[89] while the U.S. National Intelligence Council's *Global Trends 2030: Alternative Worlds*,[90] published in December 2012, speculated that, "in the event of a more fragmented Iraq or Syria, a Kurdistan would not be inconceivable"[91] and that this would constitute a "blow to Turkish integrity."[92] Some of this speculation relates to a Kurdistan carved exclusively out of Iraq,[93] and some to the prospect of a wider Kurdistan that might incorporate Turkey's southeast. Politicians and statesmen generally employ short-term perspectives, but history unfolds over a longer time scale, and involves dramatic change as well as stubborn continuity. It can involve the rise and fall of empires, the appearance and disappearance of states, chaos, and degeneration as well as order and growth and shifts in identities and perspectives. Time will tell whether we are currently witnessing the prelude to a changed order in the Middle East, and particularly with respect to the fortunes of its Kurds.[94] However, Washington would be wise to think through the implications of a potentially profound reordering of the region's arrangements.

The Syrian Uprising, Sectarianism, and the Kurdish Question.

Prior to the Syrian uprising against the Ba'athist regime of Bashir al-Assad, which turned violent in the first half of 2011, Turkey had warmly embraced the Damascus regime, perhaps inadvisably given its poor human rights record and Washington's disapproval.

Bilateral trade mounted, visa free travel arrangements were put in place, and a host of other political, security, economic, and social agreements were signed. A High Level Strategic Cooperation Council between Damascus and Ankara held its first ministerial meeting in October 2009. However, as Assad's regime responded to growing opposition with increasing violence, Ankara's approach abruptly changed tack. Turkey was disappointed that its Syrian friends did not heed their advice to respond to the frustrations of the street, and found itself confronted with a flow of refugees across the Syrian border into a corner of Turkey that contains significant Alevi, Alawite, Arab, and Kurdish minorities, thus threatening an overspill of Syria's sectarian and ethnic tensions into Turkey.[95] The May 2013 car bombings in the Turkish border town of Reyhanli that killed 43 people seemed to confirm Turkey's vulnerability to Syrian developments.[96]

Ankara was quick to take a leading role in the call for the removal of the Assad regime. It sponsored the formation in August 2011 of the Syrian National Council (SNC) and hosted it in Istanbul until it expanded and reformed as the Syrian National Coalition in November 2012, basing itself in Doha, Qatar. The SNC is closely linked to the Free Syrian Army (FSA) which is largely formed and led by defectors from the Syrian government's armed forces. Until November 2012, the FSA was headquartered in Turkey, where it is strongly rumored to have received training and arms. Turkey is also a leading light in the largely western Friends of Syria group of countries. It joined the Arab League, the European Union (EU), and the United States in imposing sanctions on the Damascus regime.

Following incidents of cross-border fire from Syria, in which two Turkish civilians were killed, and the shooting down of a Turkish fighter jet in June 2012, Turkey not only shelled Syrian military positions but also began calling for the creation of a "humanitarian corridor" in northern Syria, as a safe haven for refugees but also as a base for the FSA. In October 2012 Turkey's Grand National Assembly (NGA) voted to give the government a 1-year green light to militarily intervene in Syria should it be deemed necessary. However, once it became evident that the Assad regime was not going to crumble quickly, and also that there was little support from Turkey's NATO and EU allies for intervention, Ankara found that its rhetoric and behavior had left it in a somewhat exposed position.[97] In December 2012, NATO acceded to a Turkish request to deploy Patriot anti-missile systems close to the Syrian border. Although Ankara has since had little alternative but to align itself with Washington and with wider diplomatic efforts to find a solution to the Syrian crisis, it continues to be at the forefront of calls to arm the opposition and to establish a humanitarian corridor. It is also accommodating an influx of Syrian refugees that numbered around half a million by mid-2013.

One implication of the Syrian crisis has been the resurgence of sectarian rifts in the region, which have further damaged Ankara's relationship with Baghdad and, indeed, Iran. Iran has stood by its ally in Damascus, while Maliki too has expressed his pro-Assad sympathies. On both the Syrian and Iraqi issues, Saudi Arabia and Qatar have lent their support to the anti-regime side. Given the largely Alawite makeup of the Syrian regime, and the essentially Sunni nature of the opposition, the fact that Iran and Turkey found themselves on opposite sides has—rightly or wrongly—been interpreted as suggesting that a sectarian undercurrent is now evident in regional diplomatic alignments. Thus, a Tehran-Baghdad (and Damascus) axis is pitted in opposition to a Turkey-Gulf Arab coalition. Turkey's JDP government's evident preference for the Syrian Muslim Brotherhood faction within the SNC has added substance to these rifts.[98] Ankara's 2011 agreement to host NATO early warning radar facilities as its contribution towards a ballistic missile defense shield, widely seen as directed primarily at Iran's growing missile threat, was badly received in Tehran, which sees the Patriot deployments in a hostile light.[99] Given the Sunni roots of Turkey's ruling party, and the sense of exclusion felt by Turkey's substantial Alevi population, regional sectarian tension could have unsettling domestic repercussions in Turkey also.

Syria's minorities — Christians, Kurds, and Druze, as well as Alawites and secular Sunnis — are generally suspicious of the Arab nationalist and Muslim Brotherhood strands that appear to be dominant elements in the opposition to the Assad regime. Many of Syria's numerous Kurdish factions have come together to form a Kurdish National Council (KNC), which has as its key demand the establishment of a Syrian federation to include an autonomous Kurdish region. Although worried by the prospect of Kurdish secession in the context of Syria's turmoil, Ankara has sought to enlist KRG President Barzani in its endeavors to persuade the KNC to commit to the SNC. However, most of the squabbling elements that make up the increasingly Islamic and Arab nationalist SNC are hostile to Kurdish aspirations. In any case, Syria's Kurds are almost as divided as the SNC,[100] and although their plight under the Assad regime has been a far from happy one, some appear to distrust the Syrian opposition to Assad as much or more than they distrust Assad, and they have generally kept their distance from it.

Behind Ankara's reasoning, and that of Barzani, is the perceived threat posed by the Democratic Union Party (*Partiya Yekitiya Demokrat*—PYD), which has stayed aloof from the KNC and is seen by Ankara and Erbil alike as Syria's PKK offshoot. However, the PYD appears to enjoy the support of the majority of Syria's Kurds, and boasts a powerful armed wing. This has enabled the PYD to take control of most of the heavily Kurdish populated areas of northern Syria, an outcome eased by the withdrawal of Assad's forces from the region at an early stage in the revolt. Notwithstanding some clashes between the PYD and pro-government forces in late-2012, and the PYD's demands for Syrian Kurdish autonomy, Ankara suspects that the PYD is in an alliance of sorts with the regime, that the recent spike in PKK violence inside Turkey was linked to Syrian—and Iranian—displeasure with Ankara's opposition to Assad,[101] and that the prospect of a PKK haven opening up in northern Syria is aimed at deterring Turkish involvement in Syria's domestic affairs.

Many Turks are convinced that Damascus resuscitated its support for Turkey's Kurds in retaliation for Ankara's support for the SNC,[102] with reports that around 2,000 PKK fighters moved from northern Iraq to the Syrian border with Turkey. As it is reckoned that as many as one-third of the PKK membership is of Syrian Kurdish origin,[103] Ankara is obliged to take any such developments seriously. After all, the Damascus regime—especially in the form of Bashar al-Assad's father, Hafiz—has a track record of supporting and sheltering the PKK in its struggles against Turkey. Clashes between PYD and anti-government forces that broke out in late-2012 and early-2013 might suggest some credence to the Turkish view.[104] However, it would appear that the anti-government tribal Arab and jihadist-inclined groups provoked the clashes, and that they may have operated with the support of Turkey — even crossing from Turkey to mount their operations. Many Turks believe this; Syrian Kurds certainly do.[105] Gradually, the Kurdish issue has emerged as an even bigger worry for Turkey than the ongoing conflict between Syria's pro and anti-government forces. By July 2012, Turkey's prime minister was warning of the possibility of Turkish air strikes against PKK elements in northern Syria.[106]

Barzani shares Ankara's distaste for the PKK and PYD. He is keen to preserve his advantageous relationship with Ankara and to maintain the KRG's economic progress, is irritated by the PKK's presence in northern Iraq, and appears to genuinely believe that the JDP government in Ankara should be given the benefit of the doubt with respect to Kurdish aspirations. On the other hand, Barzani has expressed his support for the Syrian federation idea,[107] and he recognizes the disadvantages that division carries for the Syrian Kurdish cause. At a gathering of Syrian Kurds in Erbil in summer 2012, he managed to broker a united front between the PYD and the KNC.[108] His KDP has also been engaged in establishing and training a Syrian Kurds *peshmerga* that could form a fighting arm for those elements of the KNC that look to him for leadership. However, the PYD has prevented them from crossing into Syria from their northern Iraqi bases, which is just one indication of how unsuccessful Barzani's efforts to forge greater Syrian Kurdish unity have been.[109] In May 2013, the PYD arrested 74 members of an armed pro-KDP faction that apparently did manage to cross into Syria. In retaliation, Barzani closed the KRG-Syrian border.[110] Skirmishes between the PYD and other Syrian Kurdish factions have reportedly occurred on a number of occasions at least since mid-2012.[111]

Despite these difficulties, the emergence of a Syrian "Kurdish question" and the interest Barzani has taken in it has introduced a note of disquiet into Ankara-Erbil relationships. Ankara does not wish to see an autonomous Kurdish zone in Syria, and is mistrustful of the role the Iraqi Kurdish leadership might be playing.[112] On the other hand, should Syria continue its descent into "failed state" status, Ankara would prefer a Syrian Kurdish entity that is under Barzani's influence rather than that of the PKK and its affiliates, and might welcome it as a buffer zone against a chaotic Arab Syria—much as the KRG functions with respect to Iraq. Should improvements in the circumstances of Turkey's Kurds materialize, then enhanced economic, social, and even political interdependence with Ankara could prove to be an acceptable, and the most beneficial, outcome for Syria's Kurds. In short, it is not unthinkable that Syria's Kurds might arrive at arrangements not dissimilar to those enjoyed by their Iraqi cousins, with respect both to their relationship with Ankara and with their Arab neighbors.

An Iraqi Kurdistan?

Perhaps the primary threat to the KRG's current status stems from its dependence on Baghdad for around 94 percent of its budget.[113] The resentment shared by all the leading factions in Arab Iraq is putting at risk the KRG's continued receipt of 17 percent of Iraq's national budget—in fact, it already receives rather less than that. There is little doubt that Iraq's Kurds could survive on far less, but there is also little doubt that a reduction in this allocation would give them pause for thought. Even so, how realistic is it to suppose that the Kurds would step back from their bid for maximum autonomy, given their experiences of struggle and repression in Iraq? Could the KRG leadership countenance the restoration of an Arab military presence on KRG territory, and a disarming or subordination of the *peshmerga*?

With respect to Kirkuk and other disputed territories, there are as yet few signs that Iraq's Kurds are prepared to forego their claim. However, Barzani long ago softened the KRG's position on its claim to Kirkuk, at least rhetorically, by countenancing a power sharing arrangement for the city and its environs and by agreeing to give serious consideration to UN proposals for disputed areas of northern Iraq.[114] However, there has been no progress on this issue, and it remains an open question whether, over the longer term, power sharing would work any better at the local level than it has at the national level. In any case, would Baghdad become more accommodating rather than more assertive if the Kurds were prepared to concede, and how might Kurds left on the "Arab" side of the "green line" be treated? Also, given Baghdad's approach to the development of the energy resources of Arab Iraq, is it reasonable to anticipate that Baghdad would adopt a more dynamic approach to the development of the north's riches, if it was allowed the capacity to do so? What can Kurds give to Baghdad beyond supine appeasement, and what does Baghdad want from Iraq's Kurds beyond their subordination?

Of course, were Baghdad's political processes to produce a more reasonable leadership, then there could be stronger grounds for a more positive assessment of the future for Arab-Kurdish relations inside a federal Iraq. Although all leading Arab Iraqi figures would seek to limit Kurdish autonomy, an improvement on the current atmosphere would surely require Maliki's removal and the reinstatement of a power-sharing coalition in which the Kurds played a full part—as was the original hope. However, it is far from clear that this would produce anything other than resort to the blocking mechanisms, not least by the Kurds, that have plagued post-Saddam Iraqi politics from the outset. It would not follow that the territorial differences or energy disputes between Erbil and Baghdad would be resolved, or even that tension surrounding these issues would be reduced. That would necessitate a redrawing of the constitution and would probably require external pressure and guidance—which is unlikely to be forthcoming, including from Washington. On the other hand, a post-Maliki coalition Iraqi government might win Turkey over to a policy of re-engagement with Baghdad (and would presumably have the opposite effect on Tehran). This might in itself serve to isolate the Kurds, who once again could find themselves with, according to their proverb, "no friends but the mountains." Optimists about Iraqi politics—and at least in its rhetoric the Obama administration should be so counted—would presumably be content with such an outcome. But it would fail to take account of Kurdish aspirations and fears, or of Turkey's energy ambitions.

More pessimistic scenarios posit little improvement in Baghdad's politics or in Arab-Kurdish relationships in Iraq. If this stream of supposition proves truer, then the spotlight will shine on Turkey particularly fiercely. If Ankara continues to find itself faced with an uncooperative, perhaps hostile and dysfunctional regime in Iraq, how far would it go in its embrace of Iraqi Kurdistan? In an interview with *Time* magazine in December 2012 in which he was questioned on the prospects for Kurdish independence, KRG Prime Minister Nechirvan Barzani, believed by many to be the KRG's next leader, replied that:

> first of all, we have to convince at least one country around us. Without convincing them, we cannot do this. Being land locked we have to have a partner, a regional power to be convinced and internationally, a big power to be convinced to support that.[115]

That "door of hope," he said, "is Turkey. And if that door, that hope is closed, it will be impossible for us to surrender to Baghdad."[116] Nechirvan Barzani has been highly instrumental in engineering the rapprochement with Ankara, but he is far from alone among the KRGs, and especially its KDP, leadership. Another leading KDP and KRG figure, Safeen Dizayee, has said in an interview that "even if tomorrow when there is a Kurdish independent state in Iraq, it would be a dependent independent [country] whether on Turkey, Iran, Syria or Iraq," [117] and made it clear that Turkey represents the preferred option. Falah Mustafa Bakir, head of the KRG's Department of Foreign Relations, is another leading KRG figure who pins his hopes on the KRG's relationship with Turkey.[118] However, these KRG leaders understand that Turkey is not ready and may never be ready to countenance full Kurdish independence. They would also welcome a more accommodating regime in Tehran with which they could constructively engage. However, they all dismiss Baghdad as a fruitful partner, at least given the current composition of its government, but possibly existentially too.

Ankara is clearly engineering an ever-closer relationship with the KRG, even while falling far short of supporting its formal independence. The objective appears to be to create an economic, and indeed political, "interdependence" between Turkey and the KRG, both because the KRG is a neighbor that possesses energy resources and markets that Turkey needs, but also as a means to lever Baghdad. If and when Baghdad adopts a more constructive policy towards the development of the KRG's energy resources, then Iraq would support rather than oppose the geographically and economically-determined export of northern Iraq's gas and oil via Turkey[119] — an outcome that would reflect American preferences. In other words, the KRG and Turkey will economically grow together in any case, not least via energy considerations. The only issue is whether and when Baghdad will give this development a green light. This, in turn, leads back to the question of the future of Baghdad's political processes, and raises the question of what Turkey's response would be were Baghdad to continue to be a dysfunctional or hostile neighbor.

At present, Turkey's expectations of Baghdad are low. Furthermore, it has embraced the reality of the KRG's de facto independence and is maximizing the economic benefit it can obtain from the situation.[120] In aligning itself with the KRG on the issue of the legality of Erbil's energy policy, including the export of crude oil by Genel Energy, Ankara is also aligning itself, and enabling, an interpretation of Iraq's federalism that maximizes the KRG's independence from Baghdad.[121] Turkey depends on imports for over 90 percent of its (growing) oil and gas consumption. Of that, Iran provides around half of its oil and one-fifth of its gas,[122] and is the only neighboring country with which Turkey has a trade deficit. This degree of Turkish dependency on Iran is itself historically a function of the U.S.-inspired sanctions on and wars with Iraq, which had before the early-1990s been a more important trade partner for Turkey. Furthermore, Iranian gas is expensive, Tehran has proven to be a difficult trade partner, sanctions against Iran have put pressure on Turkey to find alternatives, and, in any case, Ankara's overarching policy is to diversify its suppliers. Iraq generally, and northern Iraq in particular, offers a very real energy prospect for Turkey, whose aspiration to develop as an energy hub, where energy can be stored, refined, traded, and exported, reinforces Turkey's interest in northern Iraq's rich energy resources.

So, if Iraq continues along its present path, how will Ankara square its declared commitment to Iraq's territorial integrity with its embrace of a de facto independent KRG? Given the uncertain future of its own Kurdish problem, and the likely reaction of Iran in particular, it is hard to imagine Turkey supporting an Iraqi Kurdish declaration of independence. Even so, it should be noted that in the early days of the Republic, Ankara sought to incorporate within its own borders the Ottoman province of Mosul, which included the Kurdish populated areas of what later became Iraq. In 1925, the League of Nations found in favor of British Iraq, but, at various junctures since then, Turks have revisited the terms and indeed the justice of this outcome. For example, in 1986 Ankara apparently warned the United States and Iran that it would demand the return of Mosul and Kirkuk (in effect, the former Ottoman *viliyet* of Mosul) in the event of disorder in Iraq as a consequence of the Iran-Iraq war.[123] During the first U.S.-led war against Iraq, President Turgut Ozal mused about historic Turkish claims to the region in the event of an Iraqi collapse.[124] In May 1995, Turkish President Suleyman Demirel proposed that the border should be rectified in Turkey's favor,[125] and in December 2003 expressed regret that Turkey had been denied Mosul province in 1923.[126] In August 2002, Defence Minister Sabahattin Cakmakoglu, admittedly a member of the far right National Action Party (*Milliyetci Hareket Partisi*—MHP), chose to remark that Iraqi Kurdistan had been "forcibly separated" from Turkey at the time of the Republic's formation in 1923, and that Ankara retained a protective interest in the region.[127] As U.S.-led military action against Iraq approached, Abdullah Gul's predecessor as foreign minister of the new Justice and Development Party government, Yasar Yakis, apparently sought legal clarification of the status of Mosul and Kirkuk,[128] while one of Turkey's leading commentators pointed out that Mosul and Kirkuk were ceded to Iraq, not to any Kurdish state that might subsequently emerge.[129] More recently, there have been unconfirmed reports that David Petraeus, as Central Intelligence Agency chief, raised with Turkish Prime Minister Erdogan the possibility of independence for the KRG.[130]

Turks today are fond of pointing out that Iraq, and particularly its Kurdish north, is a neighbor with which Turkey's own security is interconnected and towards which Turkey cannot be indifferent. This is not to predict that a Turkish annexation of northern Iraq is on the horizon, but it helps to be reminded—not least in the wake of the Soviet, Yugoslav, Czechoslovakian, Indonesian (East Timor), and Sudanese redrawing of state boundaries, not to mention the de facto and Turkish-sponsored autonomy of the Turkish Republic of Northern Cyprus (TRNC), and in the context of the countless territorial disputes currently raging around the world—that the territorial legacies left behind by Europe's departing colonial powers were often insensitive to demographic and geopolitical realities, and need not necessarily endure indefinitely. Nowhere is this truer than in the lands inhabited by ethnic Kurds. The march of events can bring about unanticipated outcomes, and in the Middle East in general, events are undoubtedly on the march.

A more likely outcome, and one that is not necessarily a function of the make-up of Baghdad's government, is that northern Iraq will evolve as a de facto Turkish satellite and dependency. Geography, the energy relationship, the shared transborder Kurdish ethnicity, and the sheer pull of Turkey's economic dynamism, is likely to push the KRG into the arms of Turkey, whether Baghdad resents it or not. Ambassador Riccardione's comments, outlined at the beginning of this monograph, envisage this outcome occurring via a benign process in which the entirety of Iraq economically, and maybe politically as well, aligns itself with Turkey. On current trends, this looks unlikely. Instead, the KRG's dependency on Turkey might come about as a consequence of Ankara's and Erbil's shared frustration with Baghdad, and in the face of its opposition—and presumably that of Washington, too.[131] Some Iraqi Kurds, especially from the PUK, would be uneasy about such an outcome.[132] Yet others are even prepared to speculate about a de facto or de jure "Turkish-Kurdish" federation of some kind, at least as a distant possibility.[133] There is scope for greater integration of the economies of Iraq's Kurdish north and Turkey's Kurdish southeast, and many Turkish Kurds have already benefitted from the economic opportunities across the border. The construction of the mooted gas and oil pipelines into Turkey would constitute part of this overall arrangement.

A Turkish Kurdistan?

The Turkish case is still more difficult to think through, but developments in Syria and hopes for the future relationship with the KRG have, in recent months, driven Ankara to embark on yet another domestic Kurdish initiative, dubbed the "Imrali process" because it has involved negotiations with the PKK leader, Abdullah Ocalan, who is incarcerated on a Turkish island of that name. Following a complex series of behind-the-scenes consultations, a message from Ocalan was read out at the Kurdish new year, or *Newroz*, gathering on March 21, 2013, in Diyarbakir,[134] in which he declared that "we have now arrived at the stage of withdrawing our armed forces outside the borders."[135] On May 8, PKK fighters did begin to trek through the mountains to their northern Iraqi bases — seen in Baghdad as a slight on Iraqi territory[136] — but Ocalan's address made no direct mention of what concessions Ankara had made in return. Nor has Turkish Prime Minister Erdogan been at all forthcoming, although it is for his government to initiate the next phase of the process. At the time of writing, no details of what this might look like had yet emerged.

In fact, there are few indications that the prime minister will be willing or able to meet Kurdish expectations. Although these remain largely unspecified, they are believed to include Ocalan's release or transfer to house arrest — something that Erdogan has specifically denied he has agreed to; the winding down of the so-called "village guard" system of government-sponsored and armed Kurdish citizens; the release of the thousands of *Koma Civakên Kurdistan* activists currently held in detention; a reform of Turkey's notorious anti-terror laws that are frequently used against political activists thought to be sympathetic to the Kurdish cause; education in Kurdish; establishing Kurdish as co-equal with Turkish as an official language of the Republic; the replacement of the current ethnic definition of citizenship with a civic one; an end to the 10 percent electoral hurdle for parliamentary representation; and, above all, some kind of devolution, self-determination, or "democratic autonomy" that would, in effect, introduce something tantamount to a federal political system in Turkey.[137] There appear to be few indications that Erdogan, his party, the opposition parties, or public opinion, are at all ready to concede many, if any, of these demands. Erdogan appears to think in terms of an Islamic "brotherhood" between Turkey's Turkish and Kurdish citizens, and appears not to recognize the pressure to embrace the pluralism that is inherent in Kurdish ethnic identity demands.[138] Furthermore, the behavior and rhetoric of the government during the "Gezi Park" protests that erupted in spring 2013 hardly suggested that it is set firmly on a course of further democratization, reform and inclusiveness.

Unsurprisingly, then, at the time of this writing, there is disquiet among some Kurdish leaders. In addition to impatience, voiced by Ocalan among others, at the government's somewhat tardy response in the wake of the PKK cross-border withdrawal,[139] many PKK fighters, led by their leader Murat Karayilan, have been skeptical from the beginning.[140] Indeed, Karayilan has openly expressed his doubts regarding Ankara's sincerity and has warned of the possibility of a renewed and even intensified war.[141] At the June 2013 Kurdish gathering in Diyarbakir, Ahmet Turk, a senior BDP figure, voiced similar doubts about Ankara's intentions.[142] It does indeed seem unrealistic to assume that so long and bitter a conflict can be overcome easily or quickly, and without considerable sacrifice on the government side also. In short, a satisfactory outcome to the process should not at all be taken for granted. The major obstacles are still to be overcome. A case can even be made that neither the government nor the PKK are in great need of a settlement. Each deeply mistrusts the other. The PKK remains able to recruit and raise funds, might reasonably feel that time is on its side in light of the wider developments in the region, and will seek to preserve its legitimacy. For his part, Erdogan runs the risk of incurring the wrath of Turkish nationalist sentiment, of seeming to legitimize Ocalan and the PKK, and of the initiative's failure. Nor is it necessarily the case that Ocalan, for all the status and symbolic significance he undoubtedly possesses, entertains aspirations that precisely accord with all elements of Turkey's wider Kurdish movement.[143]

The Turkish state retains the capacity to sustain a crackdown on the PKK inside its own borders and in northern Iraq. Of course, negotiations that lead to some kind of Kurdish autonomy in Turkey could also evolve, although that hardly seems to be what Prime Minister Erdogan currently has in mind. It might even transpire that Turkey's Kurds would be satisfied with little more than some relaxation of the cultural and language restrictions currently in force, which appears to be all that Ankara has in mind. Greater contact and interaction with a Turkey-leaning KRG might prove sufficient, not least as a consequence of economic benefits that might accrue. However, such an outcome would represent little return on decades of violent struggle against a very repressive and determined Turkish regime. Either the government needs to show willingness to go the extra mile in return for a lasting solution—which would probably need to consist chiefly of some kind of devolved government—or the struggle will surely continue.

If that occurs, what would the implications be for Ankara's relationship with the KRG? No doubt recalling earlier clashes with the PKK, such as during the mid-1990s, Barzani is wary of the expanded PKK presence on KRG territory that is a consequence of the "Imrali process," seeing it as a potential rival and as posing the risk of intensified Turkish military activity inside KRG territory should the process be derailed.[144] There is at least an outside possibility that failure of the "Imrali process" could result in heightened tension between Erbil and the PKK, particularly if that failure could be attributed to the PKK. This scenario would be still more probable in the event of tension between Erbil and a PYD-dominated autonomous Kurdish zone in Syria. On the other hand, should Ankara take the blame for a renewal of the struggle against the PKK and a denial of Kurdish rights in Turkey, Barzani would find himself under domestic pressure to distance the KRG from Ankara—pressure that Tehran, and perhaps the PUK, too, would seek to exploit. Turkey's relationship with Iraq's Kurds is conducted more through Barzani's KDP than through the PUK, which historically has been relatively open to Iranian influence. The KRG is by no means a unified entity. The PUK is, in general, less enamored of the KRG's new relationship with Turkey, more accommodating towards Baghdad, and closer than is the KDP to Syria's PYD.

An Iranian Kurdistan?

Iran's Kurds are at least as geographically dispersed, politically fragmented, and cowed as their Syrian counterparts have been, and are even more understudied.[145] Since 2004, Iran, like Turkey, has been in a struggle with Kurdish fighters operating from Iraqi Kurdish territory, in the form of the Party for Life and Freedom in Kurdistan (*Partiya Jiyana Azad a Kurdistane* – PJAK). Like Syria's PYD, PJAK is widely assumed to be affiliated with the PKK. In the past, Ankara has cooperated with Iran against the PKK/PJAK threat from northern Iraq. Iran also suspects that PJAK is or was sponsored by the United States as a means to destabilize the Iranian regime. Certainly during the autumn of 2011, as the American withdrawal from Iraq approached, PJAK seemed to be on the lookout for a truce with Tehran. This eased the task of the KRG officials who helped broker the first ever ceasefire between PJAK and Iranian forces, which came into effect in September 2011, following an intensified summer campaign against PJAK by Tehran's security forces.[146] However, given the KRG's autonomy, the establishment of a Kurdish self-governing zone in Syria, and the "Imrali process" in Turkey, Tehran must be feeling isolated and its ethnic Kurds left behind by the progress being made by their kin in neighboring countries. They could conceivably be inspired to emulate them.[147] Such is Iranian Kurdish disunity, however, that attempting prediction is ill-advised, although recently there have been attempts to forge greater unity.[148] In the past, Kurdish challenges in Iran have tended to materialize at moments of crisis in the country. An attack against Iran's nuclear facilities, or an implosion of the regime there, could lead to a scenario resembling that currently at play in Syria and that has created the current Iraqi situation, in which Kurdish elements could seek to exploit the chaos in order to establish some autonomy.

CONCLUSIONS AND RECOMMENDATIONS

The pathway to a fully independent and pan-Kurdish state is hard to visualize. The geographical location and the history of the Kurds, inside and outside Iraq, are unenviable. For Iraq's Kurds, in the absence of a functional government in Baghdad or of an Iran fully integrated into the regional and global system, a close embrace by an economically and politically dynamic Turkey, which can offer markets, investment, protection, and diplomatic connectedness, might not be the worst possible outcome, though it too would undoubtedly bring challenges.[149] Syria's Kurds could conceivably take a similar route. Of course, the road to any such outcome is strewn with risks and obstacles. Iran could object, but its protests might be stifled by the prize of preponderant influence in Shia Iraq. Tehran might also be appeased by Turkish and Iraqi Kurdish cooperation with respect to its own Kurdish difficulties. Baghdad, too, might be unhappy, but there would be little it could do in the face of Erbil's economic and political dependency on a Turkey determined to tighten its hold over Iraq's north. In fact, arguably a bigger risk for Iraq's Kurds would be the risk of a cooling of the Ankara-Erbil relationship as a result of developments in Syria's Kurdish lands, or of intra-Kurdish tensions that undermine the political cohesion of the KRG. It is possible — even likely — that splits within the Syrian and indeed Iranian Kurdish movements — splits that could appear in Turkey, too, if and when a political process there gets fully under-way,[150] — could magnify the divisions inside the KRG between the PUK and the KDP. If the PYD retains its current ascendency in Syrian Kurdistan and is able to use it to enhance Kurdish autonomy — both of which are quite likely — then a great deal will depend on fac-tors such as whether the PYD actively supports the PKK, whether Turkey is able to make such profound political progress that it leads to the effective disarma-ment of the PKK and the end of its violent struggle against Turkey's security forces, and whether Bar-zani — or good sense — is able to steer Syria's Kurds away from confrontation with Turkey in a manner that reassures Ankara. Much also depends on what kind of post-Assad regime emerges in Damascus and how its relationship with the country's Kurds evolves. Another possibility is that there could be some kind of fusion between Iraqi and Syrian Kurdish autonomous entities, although this, too, would depend on the for-tunes of the PYD in Syria and its relationship with the KRG.

However, it is clear that whatever transpires in Syria and whatever path the latest "Kurdish opening" in Turkey takes, the Kurds will have the capacity to deny stability to each of the countries in which they reside for so long as their aspirations are not consid-ered. This applies to Iraq as well. In the seemingly un-likely event that the Arab politics of Iraq stabilize to such a degree that a more sustained onslaught against Kurdish autonomy can be mounted, the Kurds would undoubtedly resist and a bloodbath would ensue, the outcome and ramifications of which would be highly uncertain. Would Turkey seriously intervene on behalf of the KRG, as has been rumored it might? How would Washington, which bears heavy responsibility for the state of affairs in Iraq and which is currently arming Baghdad, react? How would Tehran react? In short, in today's fast-moving regional environment, it is more difficult than ever to predict the future for the Kurds of Iraq, or indeed of the wider region. Washington's ally, Turkey, finds itself torn between its vulnerability to the turmoil in its neighborhood, and a desire to act in order to change it, possibly dramatically. However, recent developments suggest that, whatever the future holds, it is very unlikely to resemble the past. Washington will determine for itself how actively it will engage in trying to shape that future. It will be less able to choose for itself how much that future impinges on its interests and preferences in the region.

Recommendations to U.S. Policymakers:

- Be more proactive in helping resolve the KRG-Baghdad relationship, in particular with respect to agreement on a hydrocarbons law. This would enable KRG energy resources to be exported to and through Turkey.
- Encourage Ankara and Baghdad to improve their relationship, and especially to explore the possibility of a north-south energy pipeline in Iraq.
- Encourage Prime Minister Maliki to adopt more inclusive and less confrontational policies towards the country's Kurdish, Sunni Arab, and even its other Shia groups, so that Iraq can consolidate its democracy and achieve stability.
- Make rearming Iraq, especially the sale of F-16s, dependent on Baghdad adopting more conciliatory and inclusive domestic policies.
- In the event of a failure to improve relation-

ships in the region, consider the implications of its commitment to the Maliki government for U.S. relations with Turkey and the KRG, and for the development of Iraq's energy resources.
• Prepare for the possibility that Syria and/or Iraq might fragment or descend into continued chaos, thereby potentially pushing Iraqi and Syrian Kurds into the Turkish orbit.

ENDNOTES

1. See *www.turkey.usembassy.gov/amb_ricciardone_020513.html*.

2. *Ibid.*

3. *Ibid.*

4. "Turkish FM slams Maliki," *Hurriyet Daily News*, February 5, 2013, available from *www.hurriyetdailynews.com/turkish-fm-slams-maliki.aspx?pageID=238&nID=40577&NewsCatID=338*.

5. Suadad al-Salhy, "Iraq budget opens new front in Kurdistan feud," *Reuters*, February 16, 2013, available from *www.ekurd.net/mismas/articles/misc2013/2/govt2162.htm*.

6. For background and analysis of this issue, see *Iraq and the Kurds: The High-Stakes Hydrocarbons Gambit*, Middle East Report No. 120, Brussels, Belgium: International Crisis Group, April 19, 2012.

7. Hevidar Ahmed, "Iran tells Iraq's Kurds: don't think about independence or closer ties to Turkey," *Rudaw*, available from *www.rudaw.net/english/kurds/5732.html*.

8. Sevgi Akarcesme, "Ambassador Tan: U.S. rhetoric at times resembles that of Iran's on the issue of Iraq," *Sundays Zaman*, January 8, 2013, available from *www.todayszaman.com/news-303463-ambassador-tan-us-rhetoric-at-times-resembles-irans-on-the-issue-of-iraq.html*.

9. For a full list of energy companies operating in the KRG, see "Active oil companies in Iraqi Kurdistan," *Kurdnet*, January 8, 2013, available from *www.ekurd.net/mismas/articles/misc2013/1/ invest898.htm*.

10. "Minister Hawrami at Baker Institute in Houston: U.S. can help Baghdad and Kurds make fair energy deal," April 23, 2013, available from *www.krg.org/a/d.aspx?l=12&a=47315*. Also, author's interview with Mahmoud Othman, member of Iraqi parliament and former member of Iraq Interim Governing Council, London, United Kingdom (UK), May 18, 2012.

11. For an overview of U.S. policies towards the Kurds, see Marianna Charountaki, *The Kurds and U.S. foreign policy: international relations in the Middle East since 1945*, London, UK, and New York: Routledge, 2011.

12. Ofra Bengio, "Will Barzani declare independence?" *Jerusalem Post*, April 22, 2012. For a commentary on this, see *www.jpost. com/Opinion/Op-EdContributors/Article.aspx?id=267115*. For the KRG's governance system and the relationship between its two leading parties, see Gareth R.V. Stansfield, *Iraqi Kurdistan: Political Development and Emergent Democracy*, Abingdon, Oxon, UK, and New York: Routledge, 2003.

13. For further detail on earlier Turkish perspectives on the KRG, see Bill Park, *Turkey's Policy Towards Northern Iraq: Problems and Perspectives*, Adelphi Paper 374, London, UK: International Institute for Strategic Studies, May 2005.

14. F. Stephen Larrabee and Gonul Tol, "Turkey's Kurdish Challenge," *Survival*, Vol. 53, No. 4, August-September 2011, p. 144.

15. Soner Cagaptay and Tyler Evans, *Turkey's Changing Relations with Baghdad: Kurdistan Up, Baghdad Down*, Policy Focus 122, Washington, DC: Washington Institute for Near East Policy, October 2012, p. 1. Further references to Barzani will always be to President Massoud, unless specifically indicated otherwise.

16. Henri J. Barkey, *Turkey's New Engagement in Iraq; Embracing Iraqi Kurdistan*, Special Report 237, Washington, DC: United

States Institute of Peace, May 2010, pp. 10-12; author's interviews with senior Turkish and other Western diplomats, Erbil and Ankara, May 2012, and Washington DC, June 2012.

17. Lale Sariibrahimoglu, "U.S. works with Turkey to counter PKK in Iraq," *Jane's Defence Weekly,* November 14, 2007.

18. Gareth Jenkins, "A military analysis of Turkey's incursion into northern Iraq," *Terrorism Monitor,* Vol. 6, No. 5, March 7, 2008, available from *www.jamestown.org/ programs/gta/single/?tx_ttnews%5Btt_news%5D=4774& tx_ttnews%5BbackPid%5D=167&no_cache=1.*

19. "Kurds 'will fight Turkish raids'," October 19, 2007, available from *www.news.bbc.co.uk/1/hi/world/middle_east/7052566.stm.*

20. Author's interview with senior KRG figure, Erbil, May 2012.

21. This term to describe the KRG was used by Denise Natali, *The Kurdish Quasi-State: Development and Dependency in Post-Gulf War Iraq,* New York: Syracuse University Press, 2010.

22. For analysis of the Kirkuk issue, see Liam Anderson and Gareth Stansfield, *Crisis in Kirkuk: the Ethnopolitics of Conflict and Compromise,* Philadelphia, PA: University of Pennsylvania Press, 2009; *Iraq and the Kurds: Resolving the Kirkuk crisis,* Middle East Report No. 64, Brussels, Belgium: International Crisis Group, April 19, 2007.

23. "On the eve of Kurdish New Year, President Barzani delivers key address," available from *www.krg.org/a/d. aspx?l=12&a=43432.* See also Lara Jakes's Associated Press interview with Barzani, "Iraq's Kurdistan president Massoud Barzani hints at secession," *Kurdnet,* April 25, 2012, available from *www. ekurd.net/mismas/articles/misc2012/4/state6155.htm.*

24. Author's interviews with senior Turkish diplomat and KRG officials, Erbil, May 2012.

25. Sefer Levent, "Turkey strategic partner, says Iraqi Kurd premier," *Hurriyet Daily News,* May 7, 2012, available from *www. hurriyetdailynews.com.*

26. "Massoud Barzani says won't allow PKK to operate from Iraqi Kurdistan," *Kurdnet,* April 20, 2012, available from *www.ekurd.net/mismas/articles/misc2012/4/turkey3893.htm.*

27. "Barzani isn't the addressee of the Kurdish problem in Turkey: BDP co-chair," April 21, 2012, available from *www.ekurd.net/mismas/articles/misc2012/4/turkey3897.htm*; and "PKK leader says Massoud Barzani should not let AKP use him," April 21, 2012, available from *www.ekurd.net/mismas/articles/misc2012/4/turkey3894.htm.*

28. For Turkey's earlier failed "Kurdish opening," see Michael Gunter, "The closing of Turkey's Kurdish opening," *Columbia Journal of International Affairs* online, September 20, 2012, available from *www.jia.sipa.columbia.edu/closing-turkey%E2%80%99s-kurdish-opening.* For the recent initiative, see Aliza Marcus, "How Turkey can make peace with the Kurds," *New York Times,* January 15, 2013, available from *www.nytimes.com/2013/01/16/opinion/how-turkey-can-make-peace-with-the-kurds.html?_r=0.*

29. Author's interviews with senior Turkish and KRG officials, Ankara and Erbil, May 2012.

30. *Turkey's Changing Relations with Baghdad*; Mehmet Yegin and Hasan Selim Ozertem, *Turkey-Iraq Relations: From Close Partners to Adversaries,* Washington DC: The German Marshall Fund of the United States, January 7, 2013; Mesut Ozcan, "Turkish Foreign Policy Towards Iraq in 2009," *Perceptions,* Vol. XV, No. 3-4, Autumn-Winter 2010, pp. 113-132.

31. Nimrod Raphael, "Turkish and Iraqi leaders at logger heads," *Inquiry and Analysis Series* Report No. 830, Washington, DC: Middle East Media Research Institute, May 2, 2012, available from *www.memri.org/report/en/0/0/0/0/0/0/6318.htm.*

32. For an account, see *Ibid.*

33. Ipek Yezdani, "No hopes for political solutions in Iraq," *Hurriyet Daily News,* May 5, 2012, available from *www.hurriyetdailynews.com.*

34. Author's interview with Tariq al-Hashemi, Istanbul, Turkey, February 7, 2013.

35. "Iraq summons Turkish envoy again as tensions grow," *Today's Zaman*, May 17, 2012, available from *www.todayszaman. com/news-280709-iraq-summons-turkish-envoy-again-as-tensions-grow.html*.

36. "Iraq warns Turkey against violating airspace of Kurdistan," *Kurdnet*, July 17, 2012, available from *www.ekurd.net/mismas/ articles/misc2012/7/govt2041.htm*.

37. Shayma Adel, "Baghdad to rethink allowing Turkish military bases in Iraq," *Al-Monitor*, October 8, 2012, available from *www.al-monitor.com/pulse/politics/2012/10/iraq-16-turkish-military-bases-on-our-territory.html*.

38. "Iraq intends deploying troops in Kurdistan to prevent Turkish army's operations," *Kurdnet*, October 18, 2012, available from *www.ekurd.net/mismas/articles/misc2012/10/govt2095.htm*.

39. Minhac Celik, "Turkey's rapprochement with KRG should not overstep Baghdad, US experts warn," *Today's Zaman,* January 3, 2013, available from *www.todayszaman.com/news-303037-turkeys-rapprochement-with-krg-should-not-overstep-baghdad-us-experts-warn.html*.

40. Toby Dodge, "Iraq's Road Back to Dictatorship," *Survival*, Vol. 54, No. 3, June-July 2012, pp. 147-168.

41. Author's interview with Tariq al-Hashemi.

42. "Iraq's Kurdistan president Massoud Barzani hints at secession."

43. For background, see Peter Bartu, "Wrestling With the Integrity of a Nation: the Disputed Internal Boundaries of Iraq," *International Affairs,* Vol. 86, No. 6, November 2010, pp. 1329-1343; Stefan Wolf, "Governing (in) Kirkuk: Resolving the Status of a Disputed Territory in Post-American Iraq," *International Affairs,* Vol. 86, No. 6, November 2010, pp. 1361-1379; Sean Kay, "Iraq's Disputed Territories: a View of the Political Horizon and Implica-

tions for U.S. Policy," *United States Institute of Peace*, Peaceworks No. 69, March 2011; "Iraq and the Kurds: Confronting Withdrawal Fears," Middle East Report No. 103, Brussels, Belgium: International Crisis Group, March 28, 2011.

44. Jane Arraf, "Kurdish-Iraqi government talks collapse amid fear of civil war," *Christian Science Monitor*, November 30, 2012, available from *www.csmonitor.com/World/Middle-East/2012/1130/ Kurdish-Iraqi-government-talks-collapse-amid-fear-of-civil-war.*

45. Abdullah Niheli, "Kurdish forces stop Iraqi army advance near Syrian border," *Rudaw*, July 29, 2012, available from *www. rudaw.net/english/kurds/5016.html.*

46. "Wrestling With the Integrity of a Nation: the Disputed Internal Boundaries of Iraq"; "Iraq's Disputed Territories: a View of the Political Horizon and Implications for U.S. Policy." Both authors contributed to UNAMI's work on the disputed territories.

47. Isobel Coles, "Iraqi Kurdistan president Massoud Barzani says Baghdad talks last chance," *Reuters*, June 3, 2013, available from *www.ekurd.net/mismas/articles/misc2013/6/state7108.htm.*

48. Armando Cordoba, "Maliki visit to Erbil results in joint committees to resolve disputes," *Rudaw*, June 9, 2013, available from *rudaw.net/english/kurdistan/090620132.*

49. "Iraq and the Kurds: The High Stakes Hydrocarbons Gambit," Middle East Report No. 120, Brussels, Belgium: International Crisis Group, April 19, 2012, available from *www. crisisgroup.org/en/regions/middle-east-north-africa/iraq-iran-gulf/iraq/120-iraq-and-the-kurds-the-high-stakes-hydrocarbons-gambit. aspx.* Raad Alkadiri, "Oil and the question of federalism in Iraq," *International Affairs*, Vol. 86, No. 6, 2010; Matthew J. Bryza, "Turkey's dramatic shift towards Iraqi Kurdistan: politics before peace pipelines," *Turkish Policy Quarterly*, Vol. 11, No. 2, Summer 2012, pp. 53-61; Robin M. Mills, "Northern Iraq's oil chessboard: energy, politics and power," *Insight Turkey*, Vol. 15, No. 1, Winter 2013, pp. 51-62; Joel Wing, "Iraq's Kurdistan Regional Government's oil policy: an interview with Samuel Ciszuk," *Musings on Iraq*, November 6, 2012, available from *www.musingsoniraq. blogspot.co.uk/2012/11/iraqs-kurdistan-regional-governments.html;*

author's discussions with Iraqi energy analyst Shwan Zulal, Ankara and London.

50. Isabel Coles, "With or without Exxon, Iraq Kurds strive for energy autonomy," *Reuters*, January 30, 2013, available from *www.reuters.com/article/2013/01/30/us-iraq-exxon-idUSBRE90T09 M20130130*.

51. Hacer Gemici, "Turkey, ExxonMobil going ahead with gas project in Iraqi Kurdistan," *Al-Monitor*, May 20, 2013, available from *www.al-monitor.com/pulse/business/2013/05/turkey-and-exxon-explore-oil-in-iraqi-kurdistan.html*.

52. Ahmed Rasheed, "Iraq blacklists Chevron for Kurdish oil deals," *Reuters*, July 24, 2012, available from *www.reuters.com/article/2012/07/24/us-iraq-chevron-idUSBRE86N12A20120724*; Mohamad Ali Harissi, "Iraq gives Total ultimatum over Kurdish oil deal," *AFP*, August 12, 2012, available from *www.google.com/hostednews/afp/article/ALeqM5gWtZJBzCXD6vArp07rTq06HYpTV Q?docId=CNG.8a95bf6fc2dee49c9ce2778a158ef7fb.111*.

53. "US energy giant Chevron signs oil deal with Iraqi Kurdistan," *Kurdnet*, June 18, 2013, available from *www.ekurd.net/mismas/articles/misc2013/6/invest921.htm*.

54. Peg Mackey, "Iraq's Kurd oil row too big to last: Genel's Haywood," *Reuters*, September 7, 2012, available from *www.in.reuters.com/article/2012/09/07/us-genel-kurdistan-idINBRE8860K620120907*.

55. "Kurdistan says Iraq must seek approval for Kirkuk oil field upgrade," *Kurdnet*, March 27, 2012, available from *www.ekurd.net/mismas/articles/misc2012/3/kirkuk726.htm*.

56. Peg Mackey and Andrew Callus, "BP moves to front line of Iraq-Kurdistan stand-off," *Reuters*, January 17, 2013, available from *www.reuters.com/article/2013/01/17/energy-iraq-faceoff-idUSL-6N0AM8TS20130117*.

57. "Kurdistan starts independent crude oil exports," *Reuters*, January 8, 2013, available from *www.in.reuters.com/article/2013/01/07/kurdistan-crude-exports-idINL5E9C7A JW20130107*.

58. "Iraqi Kurds defend oil policy, reject BP Kirkuk deal," *Reuters,* January 18, 2013, available from *www.uk.reuters.com/article/2013/01/18/uk-energy-iraq-kurdistan-idUKBRE90H09N20130118;* "BP moves to front line of Iraq-Kurdistan stand-off," *Reuters,* January 17, 2013, *www.reuters.com/article/2013/01/17/energy-iraq-faceoff-idUSL6N0AM8TS20130117.*

59. Author's interview with senior Genel Energy executive, Ankara, May 23, 2012.

60. Palash R. Ghosh, "Iraq warns Kurdistan against striking oil deal with Turkey," *International Business Times,* May 21, 2012, available from *www.ibtimes.com/iraq-warns-kurds-against-striking-oil-deal-turkey-699345;* Joel Wing, "Iraq's Kurds' gambit on pipelines to Turkey may not pan out," *Kurdnet,* May 29, 2012, available from *www.ekurd.net/mismas/articles/misc2012/5/invest841.htm;* Shwan Zulal, "The real deal behind Turkish-Kurdish oil plans: pipe dreams or reality?" *Kurdnet,* June 22, 2012, available from *www.ekurd.net/mismas/articles/misc2012/6/state6311.htm.*

61. "Turkey-Kurdistan oil pipeline to be completed in September," *Kurdnet,* June 19, 2013, available from *www.ekurd.net/mismas/articles/misc2013/6/invest922.htm.*

62. Isabel Coles and Ahmed Rasheed, "Iraqi Kurdistan pressures Baghdad with Turkey oil pipeline push," *Reuters,* July 1, 2013, available from *www.reuters.com/article/2013/07/01/iraq-kurds-pipeline-idUSL5N0F33ZN20130701.*

63. "Turkey's dramatic shift"; "Northern Iraq's oil chessboard."

64. "Iraq 'reopens strategic pipeline'," *Iraq Business News,* December 6, 2012, available from *www.iraq-businessnews.com/2012/12/06/iraq-reopens-strategic-pipeline/.*

65. "Third oil pipeline in line between Turkey and Iraq," *Hurriyet Daily News,* April 2, 2013, available from *www.hurriyetdailynews.com/third-oil-pipeline-in-line-between-turkey-and-iraq.aspx?pageID=238&nid=44063.*

66. Tolga Tanis, "Turkey's focus 'shifts' from Syria to Baghdad," *Hurriyet Daily News,* February 1, 2013, available from *www. hurriyetdailynews.com/turkeys-focus-shifts-from-syria-to-baghdad.asp x?pageID=238&nID=40265&NewsCatID=338.*

67. *Ibid.*

68. "Iraq and the Kurds: Confronting Withdrawal Fears," p. ii.

69. Author's interviews with Turkish, Iraqi Kurdish and British officials, and senior energy consultants, Ankara and Erbil, May 2012.

70. A point made by exiled Iraqi Vice-President Tariq al-Hashemi, author's interview, Istanbul, February 7, 2013.

71. "Turkey treating Iraqi Kurdistan 'as independent'," *AFP,* August 11, 2012, available from *www.google.com/hostednews/afp/ article/ALeqM5jGm5ZuKAvm5rx6r7lHmX0jlDVlFQ?docId=CNG.0a 4e52814bdbb17f662d0a35c58373db.5c1.*

72. "Iraq expels Turkey's TPAO from energy exploration deal," *Hurriyet Daily News,* November 7, 2012, available from *www.hurriyetdailynews.com/iraq-expels-turkeys-tpao-from-energy-exploration-deal.aspx?pageID=238&nid=34144.*

73. "Iraq wants to open new chapter with Turkey: PM," *AFP,* December 6, 2012, available from *www.google.com/hostednews/afp/ article/ALeqM5gbBnRBb0ibana4hF_Mln0ZYkQ8lg?docId=CNG.19a5 f06becd20ab6e0f183d0b94b8247.471.*

74. "Iraq and the Kurds: Confronting Withdrawal Fears."

75. Michael R. Gordon, "In U.S. Exit from Iraq, Failed Efforts and Challenges," *New York Times,* September 23, 2012.

76. John Hannah, "Turkey, Kurdistan and the Future of Iraq: Time for Washington to Tune Back In," *Foreign Policy* blog, May 31, 2012, available from *www./shadow.foreignpolicy.com/ posts/2012/05/31/turkey_kurdistan_and_the_future_of_iraq_time_for_ washington_to_tune_back_in.*

77. "US says oil firms should respect Baghdad government," *Kurdnet*, August 21, 2012, available from *www.ekurd.net/ mismas/articles/misc2012/8/govt2064.htm*; "Nuland on Iraq oil deals," *Turkish Radio and television Corporation (TRT)*, January 9, 2013, available from *www.trt-world.com/trtworld/en/newsDetail. aspx?HaberKodu=3d31f4cf-fe09-4026-a320-7f4c9ae9390c.*

78. Ben Van Heuvelen, "Turkey weighs pivotal oil deal with Iraqi Kurdistan," *The Washington Post*, December 11, 2012.

79. Wladimir van Wilgenburg, "Ankara asks Washington to keep its nose out of Turkey's relations with Iraqi Kurdistan," *Rudaw*, April 19, 2013, available from *www.ekurd.net/mismas/ articles/misc2013/4/turkey4662.htm.*

80. Sevgi Akarcesme, "Ambassador Tan: U.S. rhetoric at times resembles that of Iran's on the issue of Iraq," *Sundays Zaman*, January 8, 2013, available from *www.todayszaman.com/news-303463-am-bassador-tan-us-rhetoric-at-times-resembles-irans-on-the-issue-of-iraq. html*; Serkan Demirtas, "Turkey, U.S., to hold intensified Iraq talks," *Hurriyet Daily News*, January 8, 2013, available from *www. hurriyetdailynews.com/turkey-us-to-hold-intensifed-iraq-talks.aspx?pa geID=238&nID=38575&NewsCatID=338*; Turkey defies Washington and Baghdad to pursue Iraqi Kurdistan energy ties," *Kurdnet*, February 19, 2013, available from *www.ekurd.net/mismas/articles/ misc2013/2/turkey4532.htm.*

81. Seda Kirdar, *Erbil, Baghdad, Ankara and Washington: the complex politics of Kurdish oil*, Ankara, Turkey: The Economic Policy Research Foundation of Turkey (TEPAV), August 2012, available from *www.tepav.org.tr/upload/files/1345710573-7.Er-bil_Baghdad_Ankara_and_Washington_The_Complex_Politics_of_ Kurdish_Oil.pdf.*

82. Michael S. Schmidt and Eric Schmitt, "Weapons Sales to Iraq Move Ahead Despite U.S. Worries," *New York Times*, December 28, 2011, available from *www.nytimes.com/2011/12/29/world/middleeast/ us-military-sales-to-iraq-raise-concerns.html?pagewanted=all&_r=0.*

83. "The new Iraqi air force: F16IQ Block 52 fighters," *Defense Industry Daily*, December 17, 2012, available from *www. defenseindustrydaily.com/iraq-seeks-f-16-fighters-05057/.*

84. Wladimir van Wildenburg, "Barzani suggests Baghdad might use F16s against Kurds," *Rudaw,* April 9, 2012, available from *www.rudaw.net/english/kurds/4608.html.*

85. Gonul Tol, "Turkey cozies up to the KRG," Washington, DC: Middle East Institute, May 24, 2012, available from *www.mei. edu/content/turkey-cozies-krg.*

86. Author's interview with senior western diplomats in Ankara, Erbil and Washington, May-June 2012.

87. Author's interviews with a variety of U.S. and UK officials and Turkish analysts, Washington, Erbil and Ankara, May 2012.

88. For a sample of such commentary, see Ofra Bengio, "Will the Kurds get their way?" *The American Interest,* Vol. 8, No. 2, November/December 2012; Patrick Cockburn, "A decade after the invasion of Iraq, the Kurds emerge as surprise winners," *The Independent,* February 17, 2013; David Hirst, "This could be the birth of an independent Kurdish state," *The Guardian,* January 9, 2013; Yusuf Kanli, "A Kurdish state?" *Hurriyet Daily News,* January 10, 2013, available from *www.hurriyetdailynews.com/ a-kurdish-state.aspx?pageID=449&nID=38804&NewsCatID=425;* Lyuba Lulko, "The Great Kurdistan about to be created," November 13, 2012, available from *www.english.pravda.ru/hotspots/ conflicts/13-11-2012/122791-great_kurdistan-0/;* Patrick Seale, "The Kurds seize their chance," December 26, 2012, available from *www.middle-east-online.com/english/?id=56202;* Stanley Weiss, "It's time for an independent Kurdistan," May 11, 2012, available from *www.huffingtonpost.com/stanley-weiss/its-time-for-an-independe_b_2077126.html.*

89. David Hirst, "A Kurdish state is being established, and Baghdad may accept it," *The Daily Star* (Lebanon), December 24, 2012, available from *www.dailystar.com.lb/Opinion/ Commentary/2012/Dec-24/199715-a-kurdish-state-is-being-established-and-baghdad-may-accept-it.ashx#axzz2LY2iYWi9.*

90. See *www.dni.gov/files/documents/GlobalTrends_2030.pdf.*

91. *Ibid.,* p. 74.

92. *Ibid.*, p. 131.

93. Former U.S. Ambassador Peter Galbraith advocates this. See "Better a smaller independent Kurdistan than to be stuck in Iraq forever: ex-US diplomat," *Kurdnet*, January 2, 2013, available from *www.ekurd.net/mismas/articles/misc2013/1/state6757.htm*.

94. For speculation on this, see Gareth Stansfield, "The unravelling of the post-First World War state system? The Kurdistan Region of Iraq and the transformation of the Middle East," *International Affairs*, Vol. 89, No. 2, March 2003, pp. 259-282.

95. Christopher Phillips, "The impact of Syrian refuges on Turkey and Jordan," *The World Today*, Vol. 68, No. 8/9, October 2012, pp. 34-37.

96. "Turkey warns of response after Syria border town bombs," May 12, 2013, available from *www.bbc.co.uk/news/world-middle-east-22498891*.

97. Erol Cebeci and Kadir Ustun, "The Syrian quagmire: what's holding Turkey back?" *Insight Turkey*, Vol. 14, No. 2, Spring 2012, pp. 13-21; Christopher Phillips, *Into the Quagmire: Turkey's Frustrated Syria Policy*, Briefing Paper, London, UK: Chatham House, December 2012.

98. *Into the Quagmire, Turkey's Frustrated Syria Policy*, p. 7.

99. "Iran furious over Patriot missiles in Turkey," *International Iran Times*, December 21, 2012, available from *www.iran-times.com/iran-furious-over-patriot-missiles-in-turkey/*.

100. For analyses of Syria's Kurdish politics, see Denise Natali, "Syria's Kurdish Quagmire," *Kurdnet*, May 3, 2012, available from *www.ekurd.net/mismas/articles/misc2012/5/syriakurd486.htm*; *Syria's Kurds: A Struggle Within a Struggle*, Middle East Report No. 136, Brussels, Belgium: International Crisis Group, January 22, 2013; *Who Is the Syrian Kurdish Opposition?: The Development of Kurdish Parties, 1956-2011*, *KurdWatch*, Report 8, December 2011.

101. Serkan Demirtas, "Syria supporting PKK, says intelligence report," *Hurriyet Daily News*, March 23, 2012, available

from *www.hurriyetdailynews.com/report-syria-supporting-pkk.aspx? pageID=238&nid=16699*; Cengiz Candar, "Turkey claims Iran providing logistical support for PKK," *Al-Monitor*, December 30, 2012, available from *www.al-monitor.com/pulse/originals/2012/ al-monitor/iran-turkey-shiite-sunni-pkk.html*.

102. "Syria supporting PKK"; Oytun Orhan, "Syria's PKK game," *Today's Zaman*, February 14, 2012, available from *www.todayszaman.com*; Abdullah Bozkurt, "Turkey enlists northern Iraq's help in countering threat of Syria-PKK alliance," *Today's Zaman*, March 23, 2012, available from *www.todayszaman.com*.

103. Nihat Ali Ozcan and H.Erdem Gurkaynak, "Who are these armed people on the mountains?" February 2012, available from *www.tepev.org.tr*.

104. For details, see *www.kurdwatch.org*.

105. Statement Regarding Terrorist Attacks on Syrian Kurdish Town Sere Kaniye/Ras al-Ain, National Coordination Body for Democratic Change in Syria, *Kurdnet*, January 20, 2013, available from *www.ekurd.net/mismas/articles/misc2013/1/syriakurd 726.htm*.

106. "Turkey warns it would strike Kurdish PKK fighters inside Syrian Kurdistan," *Kurdnet*, July 26, 2012, available from *www.ekurd.net/mismas/articles/misc2012/7/turkey4047.htm*.

107. Ipek Yezdani, "Syrian Kurds aim to establish 'federal state'," *Hurriyet Daily News*, February 7, 2012, available from *www.hurriyetdailynews.com*.

108. David Pollock, "Syrian Kurds unite against Assad, but not with opposition," *Policywatch* 1967, Washington, DC: The Washington Institute, July 31, 2012; "*The Kurdish National Council in Syria*," Beirut, Lebanon: Carnegie Middle East Center, February 15, 2012, available from *www.carnegie-mec.org/publications/?fa=48502*.

109. *Syria's Kurds: A Struggle Within a Struggle*, pp. 4-5, 25.

110. Wladirmir van Wildenburg, "Border arrests reveal disunity, conflict among Syrian Kurds," *Al Monitor*, May 21, 2013.

111. Wladimir van Wildenberg, "Danger of Kurdish civil war in Syrian Kurdistan," *Rudaw,* July 8, 2012, available from *www.rudaw.net/english/science/columnists/4931.html.* Also see *www.kurdwatch.org.*

112. "Turkey warned Iraqi Kurds that autonomy would not be applied in Syria: PM," *Hurriyet Daily News,* November 2, 2012, available from *www.hurriyetdailynews.com/turkey-warned-iraqi-kurds-that-autonomy-would-not-be-applied-in-syria-pm.aspx?pageID=238&nID=33802&NewsCatID=338.*

113. Denise Natali, "Who will pay IOCs in Iraqi Kurdistan?" *Al-Monitor,* February 20, 2013, available from *www.al-monitor.com/pulse/originals/2013/02/iraq-turkey-pipeline-reduce-tensions-between-baghdad-ankara.html.*

114. "Iraq Kurd prime minister says ready for power sharing in Kirkuk," *Hurriyet Daily News,* June 4, 2008, available from *www.hurriyetdailynews.com/default.aspx?pageid=438&n=iraq-kurd-pm-says-ready-for-power-sharing-in-kirkuk-2008-06-04.*

115. Jay Newton-Small, "An interview with Nechirvan Barzani: will there be an independent Kurdistan?" *Time,* December 21, 2012, available from *www.world.time.com/2012/12/21/an-interview-with-nechirvan-barzani-will-there-be-an-independent-kurdistan/.*

116. *Ibid.*

117. Barcin Yinanc, "Kurdish state has to depend on neighbors," *Hurriyet Daily News,* October 15, 2012, available from *www.hurriyetdailynews.com/kurdish-state-has-to-depend-on-neighbors.aspx?pageID=238&nid=32420.* The emphasis on Turkey was strongly confirmed in the author's interview with Dizayee, Erbil, May 27, 2012.

118. Author's interview, Erbil, May 25, 2012.

119. Tulin Daloglu, "Turkey seeks 'interdependence' with Iraqi Kurdistan," *Al-Monitor,* January 23, 2013, available from *www.al-monitor.com/pulse/tr/contents/articles/opinion/2013/01/turkey-iraq-kurdistan.html.*

120. Semih Idiz, "Turkey's new thinking in Iraqi Kurdistan," *Al-Monitor*, December 27, 2012, available from *www.al-monitor.com/pulse/originals/2012/al-monitor/turkey-kurdistan-irag-barzani.html*.

121. Necdet Pamir, "Turkey contributes to Iraqi fragmentation," *Al-Monitor*, February 20, 2012, available from *www.al-monitor.com/pulse/originals/2013/02/turkey-krg-relations-strain-future-iraq-oil-interests.html*.

122. *Turkey*, Washington, DC: U.S. Energy Information Administration, February 1, 2013, available from *www.eia.gov/countries/cab.cfm?fips=TU*.

123. Robert Rabil, "The Iraqi opposition's evolution: from conflict to unity?" *Middle East Review of International Affairs*, Vol. 6, No. 4, December 2002.

124. William Hale, "Turkey, the Middle East, and the Gulf crisis," *International Affairs*, Vol. 68, No. 4, October 1992, p. 691.

125. Michael M. Gunter, *The Kurdish Predicament in Iraq: A Political Analysis*, London, UK: MacMillan, 1999, p. 118.

126. "If Turkey had kept Mosul, there would be no N.Iraq issue, says Demirel," *Turkish Daily News*, December 19, 2003, quoted in *Turkey's Policy Towards Northern Iraq*, p. 16.

127. Nicole Pope, "Cross border concerns," *Middle East International*, No. 683, September 2002, p. 11; Jan Gorvett, "A hugely unpopular war," *The Middle East*, No. 328, November 2002, p. 11.

128. Nicole Pope, "Eyes on Turkey," *Middle East International*, Vol. 691, No. 10, January 13, 2003, pp. 14-15.

129. Gunduz Aktan, "If Iraq operation takes place," *TDN*, November 20, 2002, quoted *Turkey's Policy Towards Northern Iraq*, p. 16.

130. Alan Rawand, "Why is USA supporting a Kurdish state in Iraq's Kurdistan region?" *Kurdnet*, March 27, 2012, U.S. En-

ergy Information Administration, available from *www.ekurd.net/ mismas/articles/misc2012/3/state6034.htm.*

131. "Turkey defies Washington and Baghdad to pursue Iraqi Kurdistan energy ties," *AFP,* February 19, 2013, U.S. Energy Information Administration, available from *www.ekurd.net/mismas/ articles/misc2013/2/turkey4532.htm.*

132. For a flavor of this, see B. Mohammed, "Barzani's foreign policy risks damaging Kurdistan's interest," *Kurdish Aspect,* February 3, 2013, U.S. Energy Information Administration, available from *www.kurdishaspect.com/doc020413BM.html;* "A PUK leader warns against Turkish 'trap'," *Insight Kurdistan,* January 3, 2013, U.S. Energy Information Administration, available from *www. insightkurdistan.com/tag/tigris/.*

133. Author's interview with senior Iraqi Kurdish official, May 27, 2012.

134. For the full text, see *www.ekurd.net/mismas/articles/ misc2013/3/turkey4603.htm.*

135. *Ibid.*

136. "Baghdad government says PKK not welcome in Iraq," *Reuters,* May 9, 2013, available from *uk.reuters.com/ article/2013/05/09/us-turkey-kurds-iraq-idUSBRE9480L020130509.*

137. "Kurdish conference ends with list of demands from gov't," *Today's Zaman,* June 17, 2013, available from *www. todayszaman.com/news-318516-kurdish-conference-ends-with-list-of-demands-from-govt.html.*

138. Johanna Nykanen, "Identity, narrative and frames: assessing Turkey's Kurdish initiatives," *Insight Turkey,* Vol. 15, No. 2, Spring 2013, pp. 85-101.

139. "Government needs to move on: PKK leader," *Hurriyet Daily News,* June 17, 2013, available from *www.hurriyetdailynews. com/government-needs-to-move-on-pkk-leader.aspx?pageID=238&nID =48932&NewsCatID=338.*

140. Patrick Markey and Isobel Coles, "Insight: Hopes, suspicions over peace in Kurdish rebel hideout," *Reuters*, March 27, 2013, available from *www.reuters.com/article/2013/03/27/us-iraq-turkey-pkk-insight-idUSBRE92Q0J520130327*.

141. Tim Arango, "Rebel keeps Kurds' guns close at hand in peace talks with Turkey," *New York Times*, April 11, 2013, available from *www.nytimes.com/2013/04/12/world/middleeast/rebel-kurd-karayilan-defiant-in-turkish-talks.html?pagewanted=all&_r=0*.

142. "Ahmet Turk blames Ankara government, warns the peace talks will fail," *Kurdpress*, June 11, 2013, available from *www.kurdpress.com/En/NSite/FullStory/News/?Id=4733#Title=%0A%09%09%09%09%09%09%09%09Ahmet Turk blames Ankara government, warns the peace talks will fail%0A%09%09%09%09%09%09%09%09%09*.

143. For these arguments, see Gunes Murat Tezcur, "Prospect for resolution of the Kurdish question: a realist perspective," *Insight Turkey*, Vol. 15, No. 2, Spring 2013, pp. 69-84.

144. Denise Natali, "PKK challenges Barzani in Iraqi Kurdistan," *Kurdnet*, May 10, 2013, available from *www.ekurd.net/mismas/articles/misc2013/5/state7069.htm*.

145. For the most recent comprehensive studies of Iran's Kurds, see Abbas Vali, *Kurds and the State in Iran: The Making of Kurdish Identity*, London, UK, and New York: I. B. Tauris and Co., 2011; and Kerim Yildiz and Tanyel Taysi, *The Kurds in Iran: Past, Present and Future*, London, UK, and Ann Arbor, Michigan: Pluto Press, 2007.

146. David Enders, "Iran-Kurdish rebel ceasefire holds amid scepticism," November 7, 2011, available from *www.pulitzercenter.org/reporting/iraq-cease-fire-kurdish-rebels-iran-government*; Alex Vatanka, "Probing the reasons behind Iran's 'pre-emptive' military offensive against Kurdish rebels," *Terrorism Monitor*, Vol. 9, No. 36, September 22, 2011, available from *www.jamestown.org/single/?no_cache=1&tx_ttnews%5Btt_news%5D=38440&tx_ttnews%5BbackPid%5D=7&cHash=6557ff162fd*.

147. Jake Hess, "Iran awaits 'Kurdish spring'," *Al Jazeera*, June 29, 2013, available from *www.aljazeera.com/indepth/featur*

es/2013/06/2013627152045730568.html; Wladirmir van Wildenburg, "Iranian Kurdish Struggle Linked to Turkey, Syria," *Al
Monitor*, June 14, 2013, available from *www.al-monitor.com/pulse/
originals/2013/06/iran-Revolutionary-guard-syria.html*; Bayram
Sinkaya, "Iran cautious of Turkey's Kurdish approach," *Al Monitor*,
March 16, 2013, available from *www.al-monitor.com/pulse/
politics/2013/03/iran-cautious-turkey-kurds.html*.

148. Sakar Abdullazada, "Iranian Kurdish parties Kom-
ala, KDPI treaty is preparation for collapse of Tehran regime,"
Kurdnet, September 5, 2012, available from *www.ekurd.net/mismas/
articles/misc2012/9/irankurd881.htm*; Fuad Haqiqi, "Iran's Kurdish parties KDP, KDPI meet for the first time since 2006 split,"
Kurdnet, December 14, 2012, available from *www.ekurd.net/
mismas/articles/misc2012/12/irankurd901.htm*.

149. Joost R. Hiltermann, "Revenge of the Kurds: breaking
away from Baghdad," *Foreign Affairs*, Vol. 91, No. 6, November-
December 2012, pp. 16-22.

150. Author's interview with senior western diplomat,
Ankara, May 24, 2012.

www.ingramcontent.com/pod-product-compliance
Lightning Source LLC
Chambersburg PA
CBHW071225280526
45787CB00002B/805